10421794

What People Are Saying About …

THE LEGACY BUILDER

"When it comes to leadership, there are many books that discuss the 'Want To' of leadership—but desire is never enough. This book will give you the much needed 'How To' that is necessary to lead others, making *The Legacy Builder* a must-read for anyone involved with twenty-first-century leadership."

Clint Hurdle, manager of the
Pittsburgh Pirates MLB

"*The Legacy Builder* is a story that illustrates the wise insights Rod Olson has gained in his work with elite coaches and leaders. The engaging story will remind you of what's really important and teach you the things you need to know if you desire to leave a powerful legacy."

Mark Sanborn, *New York Times* bestselling author of *The Fred Factor* and *You Don't Need a Title to Be a Leader*

"Rod's teachings have defined our organization's culture, given clarity to our leadership, and positively impacted the performance of our company. *The Legacy Builder* is required reading for all our managers and will undoubtedly impact their lives."

David B. Storm, president and CEO
of Providence Hospitality Partners

"This book will change you. It will take many from mediocrity to excellence … whether you are a coach, business leader, or parent, *The Legacy Builder* will take you to the new levels of significance!"

John C. Bandimere Jr., president
of Bandimere Speedway

"Coach O weaves a great story that's not preachy or pushy but powerful. It's a wake-up call for all of us who may have sidelined our will to be significant in the lives of others because we're too busy trying be successful."

Mitch Jelniker, anchor for
ABC7NEWS Denver

"This is a fantastic read with a great message for anyone in leadership. *The Legacy Builder* is one of those 'buy two, give away one' books. If you're looking for wisdom, Rod Olson will help you find it in this book."

Andy Andrews, *New York Times* bestselling author of *The Noticer* and *The Traveler's Gift*

"Rod Olson is one of the greatest communicators I know. He has artfully put his thoughts on these pages that will leave no man unchanged! There is more to life ... find it here."

David Cook, author *Golf's Sacred Journey* and executive producer of the major motion picture *Seven Days in Utopia*

"Why would anyone wait to buy this book? After reading only the first thirty-nine pages, I realized it's not just another book on success ... it's a blueprint driven by real-life examples and principles that make a difference in the way we live and the things we achieve."

Jerry Moore, former head coach and three-time national champion at Appalachian State University and three-time FCS and AFCA Coach of the Year

"This book is what every coach and leader needs to read. *The Legacy Builder* is now a prerequisite for every coach in our organization … it is a must-read."

Rebecca Schloegl, president of Jeffco Youth Sports Organization

"I wholeheartedly recommend this book to those that want their life to be impactful and meaningful. To those who want to make their mark on their family, friends, marketplace, and community, this is a must-read! The principles of true leadership illustrated in this book provide a great blueprint for leaving a legacy."

Augie Mendoza, senior executive at the YMCA

the
LEGACY
BUILDER

the

LEGACY
BUILDER

Five Non-Negotiable Leadership Secrets

ROD OLSON

David C Cook®

transforming lives together

THE LEGACY BUILDER
Published by David C Cook
4050 Lee Vance View
Colorado Springs, CO 80918 U.S.A.

David C Cook Distribution Canada
55 Woodslee Avenue, Paris, Ontario, Canada N3L 3E5

David C Cook U.K., Kingsway Communications
Eastbourne, East Sussex BN23 6NT, England

The graphic circle C logo is a registered trademark of David C Cook.
All rights reserved. Except for brief excerpts for review purposes,
no part of this book may be reproduced or used in any form
without written permission from the publisher.

This story is a work of fiction. All characters and events are
the product of the author's imagination. Any resemblance
to any person, living or dead, is coincidental.

LCCN 2013937390
ISBN 978-1-4347-0574-7
eISBN 978-1-4347-0600-3

© 2013 Rod Olson
Published in association with Yates & Yates, www.yates2.com.
First edition published by Denali Press in 2011 ©
Rod Olson, ISBN 978-0-9836390-1-5

The Team: Alex Field, Amy Konyndyk, Caitlyn Carlson, Karen Athen
Cover Design: Nick Lee
Cover Image: Shutterstock

Printed in the United States of America

Second Edition 2013

1 2 3 4 5 6 7 8 9 10

041713

To the late Keli McGregor,
a real-life legacy builder,
mentor, and friend.

CONTENTS

FOREWORD

I've been around coaches and leaders my entire life, and I'm honored to call Rod Olson my colleague, friend, and mentor.

He has the heart of a teacher and the soul of a coach. He is completely dedicated to this—*and the next*—generation of leaders and coaches. When he asked me to take a look at this book, I did so eagerly.

This book speaks to real-life challenges, the speed of life, the importance of relationships, and the need for mentors and coaches to pull us to the next level. You will find yourself feeling the power of a servant leader's heart as the pages turn quickly.

When it comes to leadership, there are many books on store shelves that discuss the "Want To" of leadership—but desire is never enough.

This book will give you the much-needed "How To" that is necessary to lead others, making *The Legacy Builder* a must-read for anyone involved with twenty-first-century leadership.

I hope to be a simple man in a complex world while becoming a Legacy Builder in my professional and personal life. Make no mistake: Rod Olson knows what it takes to be a Legacy Builder, and now you will have the tools too.

Clint Hurdle

1

THE WIZARD OF OZ:
PAY NO ATTENTION
TO THE MAN BEHIND
THE CURTAIN

Lance Marshall slammed his hand down on his desk. "Is he serious with these numbers?" He scattered the papers in front of him and glared at the pages. "No wonder he didn't have the guts to email them!"

Standing before him, Terri winced but stood her ground. "If you keep shooting the messenger, she may stop showing up."

Lance's gaze snapped up at her. "This isn't about you! It's about us. All of us. This company. He can't even pretend that these represent acceptable growth. Get Bryan in here. Now!"

Terri hesitated and didn't move. "Lance, he's gone for the day."

"So he just dumped these on you and left? Coward."

"He thought it might be better to discuss them tomorrow. After you'd … considered them thoroughly."

"You mean after I cool off."

Terri pursed her lips and remained silent.

"I want him in here first thing. No excuses."

"Yes, sir." Terri turned to go, then paused. "Lance?"

"What? Another disaster needing to be discussed?"

She took a deep breath. "Perhaps. You did promise your wife you'd be home by seven. Something about Tony's birthday …"

He scowled and stared at the clock on the wall. Sleek and avant-garde, its burnished steel frame and abstract numbers reflected the rest of his office decor. Amanda had given it to him for Christmas, in hopes that he wouldn't always be late getting home. It usually failed at that task, as it had today.

Something deep in his gut tightened, hard and painful,

as he thought of Amanda's face, clouded with disappointment. Again. And Tony's.

"Go home, Terri. You've got a family too."

"Yes, sir. See you in the morning."

"I'll be here."

I'm always here.

Lance gathered the sheets of the report and stuck them into his briefcase. He'd read them tonight after everyone had gone to bed. He sent one last email, then shut down the computer. He left, his stride purposeful. He really did need to get home to Amanda and the kids, especially Tony.

Sometimes he couldn't believe a dozen years had passed since they'd rushed to the hospital, more than two months before Amanda's due date, totally unprepared for how their lives were about to change.

Lance tripped over a trash can sitting next to a desk, disrupting his thoughts and his mood. He kicked it angrily. It toppled, flinging the trash all over the floor, and hit the closest desk with a solid thud.

Lance mumbled under his breath and started to leave, then remembered that the cleaning crew came in only two days a week now, a cost-cutting measure. Snarling at himself, he squatted to pick up the litter.

Cost-cutting measures. He felt swamped by them. As a company, they were doing okay, but the pressures from the board to improve the profits dramatically, not just keep a track of steady growth, pulled at him like dogs over a carcass. After all, the profits last year had been truly spectacular. They'd moved into this new space, improved equipment, took on new clients …

Lance paused, looking at the cubicles around him, silent here at the end of the day. A far cry from the rented, open warehouse space that had housed the original company he'd started with three friends. That company had launched like a bottle rocket, in part because they'd laughed a lot and worked even more.

His mouth twisted in a half smile as he thought of those guys, teammates from his high school football team. They'd been raw, naive, and enthusiastic. He'd been their quarterback, always the quarterback, calling the plays.

C'mon, guys, just one more hour. We can get this shipment out and sleep in late tomorrow.

Right, Lance, like you ever sleep in. We're starved!

I'll go get takeout.

Chinese. Extra eggrolls.

And he'd do it. He would bring over the food on the old bicycle, passing out bags as he rode by. They'd finish the order, then run a couple of the Coach's old plays to let go of the day and laugh. The guys were gone now, moved on to new companies of their own.

They'd made a dream fly. Now all he had was the bottom line.

Lance's phone buzzed in his pocket, and he took it out.

Amanda.

He silenced it. "Why does *everyone* want something from me!"

"Why does *everyone* want something from me!"

As the garage door slid shut behind his car, Lance let himself in through the kitchen. He braced for a fight but met only silence. The kitchen and dining room lay buried beneath the remnants of a joyous celebration. Streamers hung from the chandelier over the dining table, and balloons bounced merrily around on the ceiling, lifted by helium and tossed about by the air from the floor vents. The cake sat in front of the only place at the table that didn't have a straight-back chair near it, and the chocolate delight looked as if it had been shredded instead of cut. Tony's name had been smeared, and Lance guessed that Amanda had let him play in the cake once pieces had been distributed to Connie and Robert.

Where are they?

Lance listened. The house, an open construction plan laid out with Tony's wheelchair in mind, conducted sound like an echo chamber. After a moment, he heard muted voices, which told him they were on the patio. He left his briefcase on the couch and paused at the door, watching his family having fun without him.

They clustered around a fire pit, roasting marshmallows in the glowing embers of the wood fire. Robert, his lanky frame bulked up from last year's football season, perched on a bench next to his mom. He'd received early admission to Stanford. Lance had beamed with pride when he'd heard, until he realized what it would cost.

Coach could have gotten him a scholarship. Maybe we never should have left Minnesota.

Connie laughed, jerking Lance to the present again. His only daughter was barely three when Tony was born, so she took having a disabled brother as a natural thing, as if every family had one. She helped Tony thread the marshmallow onto the straightened hanger, both of them wrestling with the effort. She positioned it in the embers, since Tony couldn't see the fire.

Amanda's hand rested on Robert's shoulder, although she watched Connie and Tony, her eyes caring and cautious.

High school sweethearts. That's how everyone introduced Amanda and Lance. True, and he'd been amazed as he'd watched her grow and mature. Working with Tony had kept her active, and he was awed by her strength, courage, and intelligence in raising all their children.

Lance slid open the glass door and put on his best Robert DeNiro imitation. "Toh-NY! Happy, happy birthday, Toh-NY!"

Tony burst into laughter and jerked spastically, sending the hanger and marshmallow soaring.

Connie lunged and caught it, glaring at her father.

"Little late for the party, Dad."

Amanda stood, admonishing Connie. "Show some respect, young lady."

"But he missed—"

"He's well aware of what he missed."

Robert watched his marshmallow burst into flames and melt off the hanger, dropping into the smoldering embers.

"Sorry I'm late," Lance said evenly as he bent and whispered again to Tony, "Happy birthday, Tony."

Tony jumped and grinned, and his hand searched across the soundboard on his wheelchair until he found what he sought, a button that spoke the word *Yes!* in a mechanical tone.

"Did you have a good time at the party?" Lance asked.

Yes! Yes!

"As a matter of fact, we all did." Connie grabbed Tony's chair and pulled it away from Lance. "Now it's Tony's bedtime. Too bad you couldn't have stopped by earlier."

"Connie." Amanda's tone sounded the warning.

"Don't worry, Mom. I'll get him started," she said. "You can finish up whenever you get done here."

With that, she turned the chair and headed both of them back into the house.

Lance watched them go for a moment, then turned to Robert, only to find that his older son had disappeared. Puzzled, Lance looked around the yard but saw no movement among the shadows.

"He does that sometimes." Amanda sighed. "He's gotten very good at just disappearing. Kinda like his father."

She turned and started gathering up the bags of marshmallows. That tight, hard pain in Lance's gut deepened.

"Amanda …"

"What was it this time? Vendor reports? New client proposals?"

A bitter taste formed in the back of Lance's mouth.

"End-of-the-month reviews," he said.

"Oh, and those are always such a surprise! Since they only occur, oh, let's see … twelve times a year, they really can't be planned for, can they? Sort of like an annual event like a birthday. Just sneaks up on you, doesn't it?"

"They're important!"

"So is this family!" Amanda replied.

Lance exploded. "You have no idea how hard I work for this family!"

Amanda stood her ground. "In fact, I do know how hard you work! I see it every day! You've always worked hard for this family. You've always worked for your dream and made our life great. But when did it change, Lance? When did it stop being the dream? When did enough stop being enough for you?"

Lance felt as if he'd been slapped. "What did you say?"

Amanda let out a long, deep breath and picked up the remaining hangers; two still had burnt marshmallows dangling from them.

"You heard me. And you may not like it, but you need to think long and hard about what happens next. Because while I still love the man I married, the one I live with now is coming apart at the seams."

Then Amanda walked away too, her words echoing in his head:

When did it stop being the dream?
When did enough stop being enough?

2

THE DECISION: GOING
BACK TO MOVE FORWARD

Lance spent more time twisting around in the sheets than sleeping that night. His mind, captured by Amanda's words and the unending cycle of work, kept buzzing. But, more importantly, Amanda never came to bed.

He missed her, missed feeling her presence beside him. Lance didn't travel much these days, and it had been a long time since they'd last slept apart. Just another sign of how far his life had spun out of orbit.

Finally, he got up around 2:00 a.m. and found Amanda asleep on the sofa in their office. The tear streaks in her makeup made his chest ache, but she looked so peaceful, he didn't want to wake her. Instead, he covered her with a throw and turned out all the lights.

Back in bed, Lance vowed he'd fix this. He might not be able to do anything about work, but *this* he could fix. Any promises he made today, he *would* keep.

He awoke to the smell of bacon and the sound of silence. As he got up, Lance realized he'd missed the kids; they had already left for school. He could catch them later. First, he knew he needed to set things right with Amanda.

Standing in the door of the kitchen, Lance paused, watching his wife work her magic with an omelet. Too often he'd taken for granted how easy she made his life. Not only did she make running the house look effortless, but she also oversaw all of Tony's therapy and doctors, as well as operating a small business out of their home.

"Have I mentioned how remarkable I think you are?"

Amanda's eyebrows arched as she slid the omelet onto a plate. "Is that the beginning of an apology?"

"As a matter of fact, it is."

She set the plate in front of him. "Please don't."

"But—"

"Not yet." She handed him a fork … then slid a manila folder over to him. "Wait until you see this. Do you remember how you always said that you could always talk to Coach, any time and any place? No matter what the problem is, no matter how hard?"

Lance nodded. "I was just thinking about Coach last night."

Amanda nudged the folder. Curious, Lance opened it … and stared. "What is this?"

"It's a round-trip ticket to Minneapolis. Then there's a car rental so you can head west out on Highway 12. I reserved a room at a new inn just around the corner from the old high school, and I called Coach last night. He's expecting you, said he'd meet with you the minute you got in."

"Amanda …"

She held up a finger. "Last night, I kinda told you I wanted you to be the man I married. That's not entirely true, and I'm sorry for yelling it at you. The man I married was loving, kind, dedicated, and full of dreams. The foundation was there, and I think Coach had a lot to do with that.

"But you were also immature, naive, and lacking wisdom in a lot of ways. You've gained all that and more. I love that about you and wouldn't go back for the world.

> "I think you've lost your foundation. I think Coach can help you rebuild it."

But I watch you struggling, and it hurts. Hurts in part because I'm not the one who can help you. You have not been happy, or even content, with anything in a long time. Not with work. Not with us." She paused. "And not with me. I think you've lost your foundation. I think Coach can help you rebuild it. Please try. For us. *For yourself.*"

Lance stared at the ticket, a glimmer of hope starting to flicker in his mind. "Let me think about it."

"Lance …"

This time he held up a finger. "I really do have to handle the month-end today, but I'll think about this. I promise."

Lance felt more relaxed on the drive to his office than he had in a long time. The idea of going to see Coach lingered in his mind, growing in strength, and the fact that Amanda would take the steps to call Coach and make the reservations emphasized how much she still cared for her husband. It relieved one fear that had nagged at him over the past few weeks as she'd grown more distant.

Lance rolled his shoulders, then reached for the coffee cup on the console. Weariness still consumed him, and he still had the month-end to complete. He tried to put Coach and Amanda out of his mind. It was time for him to kick into work mode.

Lance strode into the office, back straight and shoulders set. He nodded a good morning at Terri, set his briefcase on the desk, and booted up the computer. As he waited for the computer, he opened the briefcase and pulled out Bryan's report and the folder with the ticket. He spread his palm over the folder, the idea of the trip truly taking hold in his mind.

Pushing the thought of seeing Coach aside for the moment, he turned to Bryan's report, glancing through it again. It annoyed him just as much today as it had the evening before. Lance flipped through the pages, mumbling, "Weak, weak, weaker." He dropped it as a sound from the computer told him he had mail waiting. He opened the latest email, which was from the chairman of his board. As he read through the demands and the veiled threats, his face grew hot, and he clenched his fist on the desk.

"Terri!"

She appeared in the door frame, waiting.

"Get Bryan in here. We have to take care of this now."

She hesitated, her lips pursing as she fought back what she needed to say. She crossed her arms across her chest.

Lance stared, impatient.

"What?"

She took a deep breath. "He called in sick. He sounded horrible."

A growl of rage exploded from Lance as he slammed one fist on the desk. Terri jumped, wincing, and took a step back, glancing over her shoulder as if she were about to bolt.

Lance pointed at her.

"Call him. Tell him if he's not in here by noon, he needn't bother coming back. At all. Ever."

Her eyes widened. "He's your best rep! You can't fire him for being sick!"

He grabbed the papers and flung them around the office.

"I can fire him for being incompetent!"

Terri backed away, then disappeared.

"Unbelievable!" Lance turned to his window and placed his palms against the glass, leaning heavily against it. His shoulders tightened, and he closed his eyes, wishing he could push away the pressure that had settled across his neck.

Lance let out a long breath, took another in, and opened his eyes, looking out across the parking lot. His entire world felt as if it had been jarred off its axis.

You have not been happy, or even content, with anything in a long time. Amanda's words.

His entire world felt as if it had been jarred off its axis.

He's your best rep. Terri's words.

Lance turned back to his desk, his gaze falling on the folder. He stared at it a few moments, then bellowed, "Terri!"

She appeared instantly in the doorway. "Yes, sir?"

"Don't call Bryan."

Her face brightened. "I was hoping—"

"Call all my appointments for the next week and cancel them."

"Sir?"

"I'm going out of town for a few days."

"But the month-end—"

"Can wait."

Terri stared at him, then her eyes narrowed in suspicion.

"Are you okay?"

Lance looked at his watch. Amanda would be at a school meeting with Tony, but that was fine. He'd leave her a note.

"No," he said. "But I will be."

He slipped the trip folder back in his briefcase. "There's a note from the chairman in my inbox. Would you please respond that I've been called out of town? Then shut everything down and lock my door."

"You will … you will be back?"

He picked up the case. "Yes." He headed for the door, pausing to touch her arm. "Promise."

Lance packed, fixed a bit of lunch, then wandered around the house, waiting to see if Amanda would return. He stopped in each of the kids' rooms, startled at how much had changed since he'd been in them last. In Connie's room, posters of skinny young pop singers had been replaced by images of stocky rock and country artists. A magazine page featuring a model in a purple formal had the words *PURRFECT PROM!* scribbled across the top. Tony still loved Stevie Wonder and Disney movies. Robert apparently admired Peyton Manning, Tim Tebow, and Drew Brees, although a poster of the top ten quarterbacks of all time took center place over his desk.

"Never forget the classics," Lance murmured with a grin.

He finally left Amanda a short note of love and thanks.

The drive to the airport ran right by the high school, and Lance stopped at the football field. Stepping up into the bleachers, he sat and watched the team work, listening to the coaches calling out to the players. The sights and sounds felt so familiar, Lance wondered if he could still play. The game called to him like nothing else.

Robert exchanged passes with one of the assistant coaches, warming up, backing up a little with each throw. The team had done well this year, and a twinge of regret made Lance shift uneasily. He'd been to only one game. They had only three left in the regular season, but they might go to the playoffs.

He has a good arm. He sure can spin it.

The ball traveled sure and true, even as the two increased the distance between them. Regret slipped into a sense of pride.

"I want this back," Lance whispered. "Show me how."

Robert paused for a drink of water. Turning, he spotted his father in the stands and froze. After a moment, he took off his helmet and shaded his eyes against the afternoon sun.

He probably thinks I'm a mirage, Lance thought.

Lance raised his arm in greeting. Robert held still a few moments, just staring, until the coach called to him. Then he quickly raised his arm in return before turning his focus back to practice.

"I want this back," Lance whispered. "Show me how."

Lance headed back to the car and sat, overwhelmed by how hollow and empty he felt and how consumed he was by an unnamed anger at the world. Then he picked up the phone and dialed a number he'd never forgotten, even after twenty-seven years.

"If you're still sure, I'm on my way."

3

"Coach": The Legacy Builder

Driving Highway 12 west out of Minneapolis, a route he'd not taken in almost twenty years, Lance felt as if he were rolling back time. When he first left the airport, he searched through the satellite radio stations until he found some classic rock, and with the tunes playing he slipped further into the past. As the city fell away, he examined the passing landscape, amazed at how much had changed— yet how much had stayed the same, especially as the route took him into his hometown.

The speed limit dropped to forty-five, then thirty, and he turned off the radio and lowered the windows, despite the brisk air of autumn in Minnesota.

It refreshed his spirit.

He found the inn Amanda mentioned, checked in, and put his luggage in the room. He could see the high school from his second-story window, so he decided to walk the short distance over. School had let out earlier, and kids cluttered the streets, running back and forth, tossing or kicking balls about, their shouts and squeals like music. *Small-town America*, he thought. *Gotta love it.*

Football practice was over, and he passed a few of the players as they drifted away from the school, their bodies still flushed red from the exertion, sweat plastering their hair to their scalps. A few walked with girls, who seemed to have a love-hate relationship with the way their boyfriends looked and smelled. They'd walk by their sides for a bit, then wrinkle their noses and step farther away. Lance laughed under his breath, remembering Amanda doing the same.

Ew, why don't you shower in the locker room?

It's easier at home. I can just shower and fall into bed. You don't love me when I smell?

I love you all the time, silly. I just don't like you when you're smelly and clammy. Don't you touch me!

They'd grown up together, started dating when they were sixteen. Lance had never wanted to be with anyone else.

You've got too much to lose to keep messing it up.

Lance pulled open the front door of the school and spotted his own face staring back at him. Framed photos from the glory days of the '70s and '80s ranged across the back wall of the lobby. Photos from the '50s and '60s covered a wall to the left, and those of the '90s and 2000s were on the right and down the main hall.

He paused and stared at a photo of his much younger self, his straight, thin body in midair, stretched across the goal line. He remembered that moment, a postseason playoff bid and an ill-advised choice that had almost cost them the game. He had dropped back to pass, then decided, probably too quickly, to pull the ball down and run. As he approached the end zone, he leaped into the air as a defensive lineman dove at his legs. Then just as he reached for the goal line, the meanest linebacker in the league hit him from the side, spinning him in midair like John Elway in Super Bowl XXXII versus the Packers.

But they'd won.

Lance grinned. He'd always done anything possible to win.

He headed on down toward the locker room, wandering through a strange maze of hallways. Coach always said that their high school hadn't been planned so much as grown. Wings built to accommodate the growing town branched off in odd directions. Only the gym and locker-room areas had remained unchanged. As he neared them, Lance's steps slowed, and he looked over the trophy cases lined up outside the gym. The gold and dark wood of the trophies sparkled even though they were crammed into every nook and corner of the cases.

He'd always done anything possible to win.

Most of the prizes had come to the school because of Coach. He'd started coaching just out of college, back in the '50s, and he'd trained thousands of young athletes. When Lance had attended, the Coach's emphasis had been football and baseball. But he'd branched out into girls' soccer, track, and basketball in later years.

The sport, in the long run, didn't really matter as much as coaching the kids themselves. Lance paused and looked at the slowly tarnishing award that represented his first state championship. The first of three. Starting quarterback as a sophomore, which was almost unheard of, but Coach believed in him and had given him the tools to win.

"Oh, the talent is his. I'm just building the foundation to grow it."

When a reporter once questioned the youth of his quarterback, Coach had just replied, "Oh, the talent is his. I'm just building the foundation to grow it. You think he's good now. Wait two years."

Two years. Lance grinned. His senior year, they'd gone 11–0 for the regular season. They went all the way to the state championship. The next year, he headed to an out-of-state college with a full scholarship, and Coach was well on his way to becoming a Minnesota sports legend.

"Lance?"

Lance turned.

"Lance Marshall, it *is* you! Coach Moore said you might drop by, but I didn't know whether to believe it. After all, it's been what—twenty-five years?"

"Twenty-seven." Lance grinned and held out his hand to Coach Doug Dawson, who'd been Coach's assistant for at least thirty years. "Good to see you, Coach Dawson."

"You, too! I didn't know if I'd recognize you, but you haven't changed all that much."

"A little grayer. Not as thin as I was then." Lance jerked a thumb over his shoulder at the trophies.

"Who is?" Coach Dawson asked, patting his stomach.

They both laughed since Coach Dawson, if anything, was thinner than he'd been thirty years before. Back then he'd been lanky. Now he was downright pole-like.

"Come on back to the offices. Coach and I were just finishing up a review of today's practice, but we're mostly done. I know he's anxious to speak with you."

"I appreciate him taking the time, believe me."

Coach Dawson pushed open a door leading into a long hallway. "Oh, he does it all the time. You wouldn't believe the kids that come back to talk to him. You know he and Gail never could have any children of their own."

Lance followed, the smell of the locker room hitting him immediately. "Yeah, I heard."

"But you'd think they had adopted several hundred the way they keep coming back here, showing off the kids, grandkids. Sometimes just to tell him what they've accomplished lately. And a lot of the kids he's coaching now belong to the ones he coached fifteen, twenty years ago."

"Life in a small town," Lance replied. The scent in the hall sparked even more memories, and they rushed over Lance like a flood.

"You got that right. You have kids, Lance?"

"Three. Two boys and a girl."

A memory returned to him of Amanda at his side during the pregame homecoming celebration.

Don't stand too close.

I have to escort you out. Besides, I'm not sweaty yet.

No, but you smell like the locker room.

I like the locker room.

I know. Curse of a girl who loves a football player.

"Any of them play sports?" Coach Dawson paused halfway down the hall and pushed through another door into the coaches' office suite.

"My oldest, Robert, plays football."

Coach Dawson grinned. "Quarterback?"

"Of course."

"Coach! Look who I found wandering the halls."

The coaches' suite consisted of a small anteroom, three offices, and a meeting room. The anteroom and the offices of the two assistant coaches were in good shape and relatively neat, especially considering they'd been the home of the football team for more than fifty years.

"Come in, Lance! Come in!" Coach Moore said.

The office of the man who'd been the coach for most of those fifty years was cluttered and appeared disorganized. The man who stood as a legend in Minnesota sports, however, told a different story. Coach Moore stood up and stepped over two stacks of paper in order to come from behind his desk and greet Lance. Behind Coach's desk chair, a bookshelf overflowed with playbooks, film canisters, videotapes, and DVD cases. On the far wall, a haphazard stack of files sat atop an ancient filing cabinet. Nothing was labeled, marked, or titled. But Lance remembered that if you asked Coach for something, he'd go to the right stack and pull it out for you.

"Lance Marshall!" Coach pulled Lance into a bear hug, then held him at arm's length to look him up and down. "You've aged well!" He released Lance and stepped back. "Physically, anyway. Not surprised about that part. And we haven't had a QB as good as you were since you graduated. You are one of a kind." He turned and moved a stack of papers from a chair to the floor. "Welcome back to my organized chaos. Have a seat!"

"Thanks." Lance sat as Coach moved back behind the desk. Nearing eighty, Coach was thicker and slower than Lance remembered, but he stood ramrod straight and had a clear, aware expression on his face.

"I have to admit surprise that you're still coaching."

Coach chuckled. "Lots of folks think I should retire, but, to be honest, son, I don't know what else I'd do. Don't like golf. Not fond of card games."

"Is Gail still teaching?"

Coach waved his hand dismissively in the way old men do. "Been out of the classroom more than twenty years. She's a master gardener now. And she *sure* doesn't want me around all the time."

"That can't be true."

"You just ask her. She wants you to come to dinner before you leave."

"I'd love to."

Then, small talk finished, both men fell silent. Coach leaned back in his chair, watching Lance. Lance leaned forward, resting his elbows on his knees, and stared down at his hands.

Finally, Coach cleared his throat. "So. Amanda phoned."

Lance nodded.

"Son, why don't you start with why your wife called me instead of you."

4

Coached Up: Five Non-Negotiables and One Rule

Lance told Coach about the basic issues, then leaned back in his chair.

"It took me a long time to see it," he continued. "But I feel like I've been shoved out of the game. I can't see downfield anymore, like I'm acting—*or reacting, actually*—blindly."

Coach nodded. "Amanda said you acted like a stranger in your own home."

Lance grimaced. "I'm a stranger in my own skin."

The older man reached for a baseball in an open desk drawer and turned the well-worn ball in his hands, examining it as if he were seeing it for the first time. "Angry a lot?"

"All the time. My own employees are afraid of me."

"This may have happened because things came so easily to you."

Eyebrows arched, Lance sat forward, a flash of anger running through him. "What?"

Coach put the ball down. "You don't think that because you worked so hard. But, Lance, you worked hard *perfecting* your skills, your technique in the game. You had a deep-set talent, so you never worked hard *learning* the basic elements. So when you stopped practicing, they went away." He paused. "Ever think you could just step into a game and run the plays, even today?"

"Of course. What player doesn't?"

"A smart one."

Lance froze, working hard to press down his growing anger.

"And … now you're angry with me, when all I've done is point out the obvious. Age changes a man. That's a basic fact. Believe me, I know that all too well. Learned it the hard way. You're older, heavier. Your joints are stiffer, reaction times slower, memory duller. But because it came so easily to you as a kid, you think it still should be easy."

Coach stood, moved some books, and perched one hip on the edge of his desk.

"I always taught my players, of whatever sport, the five non-negotiable principles of sports. You listened, but you didn't learn them. You walked through them on instinct, never getting out of line because that was your nature." He paused. "Think of it this way. Many times, gifted students absorb facts and figures like a sponge. They have great memories, good reasoning. They get all As because they *get* the material without studying. But, eventually, usually in high school or college, they hit a wall, as if their brains reach a saturation point. Now to continue, they have to actually study.

"The five non-negotiable principles of sports. You listened, but you didn't learn them."

"But most of them don't know how. They didn't have to study, so they never developed good study habits. They don't know how to plan, how to work ahead. They wind up writing papers the night before they're due and cramming for exams.

"This will be the pattern for the rest of their lives if they don't change it. That's why a lot of talented students never reach their full potential. You were like that in sports, Lance. You didn't see that those non-negotiables weren't just about football. They were about life."

"And now I've hit a wall," Lance said.

Coach stood and returned to his chair, nodding. "Now you've hit a wall. When you four boys started that company, it was like a continuation of high school and college. You drove it, remaining in control, the quarterback who could see far enough downfield to guide the team.

"Now you're not. Life has forced a harsh reality on you, and you don't have the foundation to deal with it. Fortunately, you have a wise wife … and you've instinctually realized something's seriously askew."

The anger had eased in Lance, and he sat straighter, suddenly understanding why: Coach was giving him a game plan. "I need to start over."

Coach nodded. He stood and motioned for Lance to follow him. They went into the locker room, where Coach thumped one of the lockers without pausing.

"Lance, you need to suit up and decide what kind of leader you want to be."

At the end of the room, they pushed through a door that led into the tunnel to the stadium. They emerged, and Lance felt the last warmth of the afternoon sun on his face. They turned onto the

"You need to suit up and decide what kind of leader you want to be."

track circling the field, their shoes crunching roughly on the surface. In the far end zone, a young man wearing only sweats bounced on his toes, took aim, and fired the ball off into a practice net.

"He's pretty good," Lance murmured.

"He works hard. He does this every afternoon except right before a game."

"Like I used to do."

Coach coughed. "No. You never worked this hard. You didn't have to. But it's also why you never went beyond college."

Lance stopped, staring at him. "Are you kidding me?"

Coach shook his head. "No. Pro scouts look for drive and ambition as well as talent. Dedication as well as love of the game. Football had been a relatively easy path for you, and they saw that."

"I'm not lazy."

Coach turned. "I'm not saying you were ... *or are*. You've hit a wall." He crossed his arms. "Look, we're describing you, but most people hit a wall sooner or later. The only people who don't are the ones who stop trying, stop achieving. They settle for something less than extraordinary. Our friend out there with the ball will eventually hit that wall as well, but his path will be different. It happens when you're overworked, make a wrong choice, find yourself under too much pressure. You lose your vision for life, feel too many people pulling at you, always wanting something, and you just want to quit and stare at the stars for a while."

"I need to start over."

"You need to rebuild your foundation. It won't be easy, just necessary. But you're not alone."

Lance let out a long breath. "I have no idea where to begin."

Coach uncrossed his arms and walked again, their steps releasing the pungent scent of the track. "After I talked to Amanda, I took the liberty of setting up five appointments for you."

"With whom?"

Coach waved his hand. "We'll get to that later. Each one is highly successful in his field. They're smart and grounded. Each is going to share one of the five non-negotiables with you, talk about how it's worked in his life, and give you a task. The goal in this is to have you learn the principle this time, and reinforce it by doing it."

"The goal in this is to have you learn the principle this time, and reinforce it by doing it."

He stopped, his face somber.

"Lance, I'm serious about this part, which is why I'm not telling you who you'll meet with until it's time to show up. You will have twenty-four hours to put each principle into action and tell me the results. If you don't, we'll stop the journey, the meetings, right then and there. Understand?"

Deep inside, Lance wrestled hard with the idea of turning the next few days over to Coach, no matter how much he trusted him. But he also realized that if he didn't do this, he'd risk everything he cared about. Ego warred with common sense.

"Yes, sir, I understand."

"So you're game? You agree?"

Lance paused, but common sense won. "I agree."

"Good!" Coach grinned and slapped him on the shoulder. "Go back to your room. Get some rest. I'll call you early in the morning with your first instructions. Oh, and I recommend Dottie's Café over on Main for most of your meals. Almost like home cooking, and she makes a mean omelet."

* * *

Back in his room, Lance undressed and showered, Dottie's meatloaf settling nicely in his stomach. Just as he was about to turn on the evening news, Lance's cell phone buzzed, and he checked the caller ID.

Amanda.

Lance answered it, suddenly realizing that for the first time in years, he was eager to tell his wife about his day.

5

Keli: Specify the Win

The First Non-Negotiable

Dottie's omelet, in fact, exceeded Coach's description, and Lance felt energized afterward, eager to dive into the day. He'd just returned to his room when a text arrived with Coach's instructions. Lance stared at the phone a moment, not really believing the name of today's contact. But the appointment was set for ten thirty, so he hit the road quickly.

Keli. Lance remembered him—or rather, he remembered the boy he used to be. Keli had been a couple of years behind Lance in high school and hadn't reached his full potential by the time Lance graduated. But under Coach's tutelage, that had changed in great measures. Keli had been an All-State tight end, played for one of the top colleges in the country, then enjoyed a short career in the NFL.

Lance stared up at the building as he approached it, feeling slightly intimidated by the name of the major league franchise emblazoned across the top. When he gave his name to the security guard at the front desk, the guard nodded and made a quick call. Moments later, a lovely woman in her midfifties stepped off the elevator and motioned for Lance to follow her.

"He's expecting you," she said simply. "Coach called him yesterday."

When the doors opened on the executive floor, Lance stepped out onto carpet so plush it cushioned each step and helped mute the sounds of an active office environment. The woman nodded and smiled as she passed people in the hallway. They turned a corner and headed toward two large mahogany doors. She opened both at once and led him inside.

Lance bit his tongue to keep from exclaiming, "Wow!"

Scents of rich wood, luxurious leather, and fine cigars greeted him in a room of masculine elegance. The deep tones of mahogany and cherrywood held tastefully placed accents of brass. Despite the dark furnishings, the room glowed with light from the tall windows, which overlooked a carefully landscaped lake circled by a walking track.

"Mr. Marshall," the woman announced.

Keli rose from behind an expansive desk that matched his six-foot, eight-inch frame. "Lance!"

With that acceptance, Lance's escort nodded and left. Keli came from behind the desk, looking as fit and trim as he had been in college. He embraced Lance with a bear hug, and then backed off to look at him. "Yep, Coach was right. But he always is." He motioned at the two leather sofas in front of tall bookcases. "Let's sit here. I hate talking to people from behind a desk."

Lance sat. "Coach was right about what?"

Keli grinned. "Life has been good to you, but you're looking a little worn down. When was the last time you worked out?"

"It's been a while," Lance admitted.

"Since the buyout?"

Lance's eyes widened, and Keli chuckled. "Coach keeps up with all his kids, especially the ones who had the greatest potential. We still have lunch about once a month. He told me when that overseas conglomerate made you an offer you couldn't refuse. You're still in charge, but …"

Lance's mouth twisted. "Not as much as you might imagine."

Keli spread his arms wide. "Trust me, all this luxury comes with a lot of accountability. Being the president of a franchise like this means answering to a lot of different folks, far beyond the players and ticket holders. I know about having someone, or a few someones, breathing down your neck. That's why I asked you when you'd last worked out." He leaned back and crossed his legs. "For a guy like you, that tells me you're out of balance."

Lance's eyebrows arched. "Balance?"

"It's one of Coach's principles. In order to reach your greatest potential, your life must be in balance. When it's not, you lose sight of what's really important. The end, the results, the bottom line becomes your goal and your priority, especially when someone's shoving you from behind."

"But those are the priorities in business."

Keli shook his head. "The bottom line is only one of the *goals*. It shouldn't be a priority." He leaned forward.

"Look at it this way. One of my goals here is to win games. But if that's all I focus on, I forget that winning is a destination with many paths. To win games, I need to build a sustainable organization, one that makes sure everyone in the organization feels safe, secure, and significant. I have to be sure all our employees and players are in balance professionally and personally. That means hiring the best coaches I can find, with philosophies of coaching and life that dovetail with each other. By focusing on the care of the individuals in the club, by focusing on the process instead of just the results, I control the pace here, instead of letting it control me. When I provide the tools, the incentive, and the care, our team wins games. The desired end comes out of the process that is executed one day at a time."

"That's not exactly what we were taught in business school."

Keli laughed. "No," he said. "They'll teach you 'the devil is in the details' and to write another business plan. Which is true, but that's just the beginning. True leadership is about inspiration and encouragement, as well as coaching ... and *balance*. Balance goes hand in hand with maturity, and it crosses all aspects of your life—mental, spiritual, physical, and emotional. And being in balance as a man and a leader means providing yourself with the same tools that you should provide for those around you." Keli stood. "Coffee?"

Lance nodded, and Keli slid open a door in one of the shelves, where a coffee service waited. He poured two cups, then returned to the couch, handing a cup to Lance.

Keli took a deep breath and continued. "Coach taught me that one way to maintain your balance in life is to 'specify the win' for each day. Decide what I want to achieve each and every day. And just for that day: *one thing at a time, one day at a time*. It is my job as the leader to always work with the end in mind, but I can't let myself or my

"Balance goes hand in hand with maturity, and it crosses all aspects of your life—mental, spiritual, physical, and emotional."

people get distracted by the future. We teach our people to focus on what a 'win' is for them personally, each day at work. However, it's not just for work. To keep your life in balance, you need a 'win' for work and a 'win' for home. If you can do that and just take one thing at a time, one day at a time, then you can control the pace instead of letting the pace control you."

Keli paused and sipped his coffee. "You can't imagine how important this is, Lance. We get so focused on what's out there, those envisioned 'results,' that we forget how to get there. We become so results driven, we forget about how important the process of getting there is. When was the last time you lost your temper with an employee?"

Lance started. "Yesterday."

"Why?"

"His month-end reports were inadequate and sloppy."

"Why? Has he performed this way before?"

"Not until a couple of months ago."

"Why did his work change?"

Lance hesitated. "I don't know."

"Why not?"

Lance felt slightly chagrined. "I guess I never asked."

Keli put down his cup. "Lance, one of my best employees was fired from a previous job because he was going through a divorce. His boss had told him to keep his personal life out of the office. But we're all human. It's not healthy to be compartmentalized. Hasn't your work sometimes interfered with your personal life and vice versa?"

Lance couldn't help but think about Tony's birthday party … and the work he'd missed when Tony was born. "Of course."

"This is why having a sense of balance with your priorities, an understanding of how important the process is, will keep you moving forward. If you stay results driven, moments of crisis will make you feel like a failure because they interfere with the bottom line. If you see them in balance, as part of

"If you stay results driven, moments of crisis will make you feel like a failure because they interfere with the bottom line."

the process, then you can work through hard times with a different view of success."

Keli stood suddenly and walked to his desk. Opening a drawer, he pulled out a baseball, so new and polished that its leather reflected the light from the windows. He tossed it at Lance, who caught it easily. "What's this?" Lance asked.

"Another thing Coach taught me." Keli sat in front of Lance again. "He has one of these in his desk too."

Lance thought about the baseball he'd seen Coach turn over and over in his hands yesterday. "What's it for?"

"On one side, you write your daily 'win' for your work. On the other, for your home. Don't think of them as personal and professional aspects. And they're not tasks. They're your life. Completely."

Lance stared at the baseball in his hand, suddenly feeling even more out of balance. "My life is all about performing tasks and getting results."

"No wonder Amanda called Coach."

Lance looked up, a sharp retort on his lips, but then he saw Keli grinning at him.

"I guess my 'team' didn't end with high school."

Keli stood. "Now you're talking. Oh, and one last thing. Remember things that are built to last are not built fast. God bless ya, brother, and call me if you have any questions about any of this."

"I will."

Lance drove back to the inn, the baseball perched in one of the drink holders. "What am I going to do with you?" Remembering Coach's admonition to put each newly learned principle into effect within twenty-four hours, he knew he'd have to decide on his daily wins soon.

> "Remember things that are built to last are not built fast."

Back in his room, he turned the ball over and over in his hands, thinking about the last few weeks at home and the office. The disappointment on his children's faces. On Amanda's. The way Terri jumped when he called her, how she'd defended Bryan.

A sudden realization hit him like a hard slap. *She knew.* Terri knew what was going on with Bryan. She knew … and he didn't. Why hadn't they told him?

Because they believe you don't care. The thought stung. Of course he cared.

But how long has it been since you've shown them?

Pulling a pen from his pocket, Lance wrote on one side of the ball: *that they know I care more about them than the bottom line.*

He sighed, looking at the words. *Now … how do I put that into practice?*

Before he could think of an answer, his phone vibrated on his belt. He checked the caller ID and grinned. Amanda. Eager to share his day's visit with her, he answered, expecting a pleasant greeting from his wife.

Instead, he heard the words he dreaded most.

"Lance, I'm at the hospital with Tony."

6

TONY: A WAKE-UP CALL

Lance called Coach as he headed for the airport. "His shunt failed. Amanda sounded terrified." Lance had a hard time keeping the fear from his own voice. "It's bad this time."

"Gail and I will be praying," Coach responded. "Others will be too."

Lance knew that Coach was a man of great faith, but the simple declaration caught him off guard. He hesitated, unsure of what to say. Finally, he said simply, "Thank you."

Coach's voice strengthened. "He'll get you through it, son. No matter what."

Lance hung up, the words echoing in his mind. *No matter what.* He didn't want to think about that part, about how often malfunctioning shunts turned fatal. He thought about Amanda, alone with Tony, and Lance had to fight a sense of deep-seated panic. They'd worked so long and hard with Tony. Born more than ten weeks early, Tony had arrived weighing barely two pounds and fighting a boatload of problems. The doctors had given him less than a 20 percent chance of surviving. His son had started life hooked up to a plethora of cords and tubes, and even a preemie diaper dwarfed his little body. Then the surgeries started.

But Tony survived. And he'd grown into one of the strongest members of the family. Blindness had sharpened his hearing, and music kept his world hopping. Cerebral palsy kept him from walking and talking, but his mind had an unexpected sharpness that charmed anyone who met him. He and Connie were best friends, and he listened to all her teenage angst, then made her laugh. She fed his music habit, and last year, she'd bought him an audio dramatization of the Bible, and they'd spent hours listening to it.

Tears blurred Lance's vision. He blinked them away and kept driving, trying not to think about how he'd pushed all three of his children away. Instead he called

Amanda, who could barely talk. "It's completely failed," she whispered. "The buildup of fluid and the infection is worse than they thought, Lance. They've taken him to surgery, but they're not hopeful."

A spike of fear shot through Lance again, and he tensed every muscle to keep from screaming. Instead, he tightened his grip on the wheel and forced the words out. "I'll be there as soon as I can."

Far too many nightmarish hours later, Lance opened the door to Tony's hospital room. Only one soft, reflective light illuminated his son, who was back from surgery, and his wife, whose head was bowed. Her hands clutched a Bible, and her lips moved silently. Tubes and wires stretched out from Tony's body, monitoring every aspect of his life, reminding Lance of those tense, harsh moments following his birth.

"Amanda," he whispered softly.

She was up and in his arms before he could take a breath. He held her tightly as she pressed her cheek against his chest, clutching his suit coat with both hands. "I'm so scared!"

"Me, too." Lance stroked her hair. "What are they saying now?"

Amanda looked up at him. "Same as always. The surgery went well, but the next few hours will tell." She shook her head. "I've been watching the nurses, watching their faces. They don't have a lot of hope."

"He has to make it. He has to."

She touched his cheek. "I know." Amanda stepped away and tugged at his arm. "Come sit with me. You've got to be exhausted." She gave him a soft smile. "I know how much you love flying."

They sat, and Lance wrapped an arm around her, pulling her close. "Yeah, right." His eyes focused on Tony. "I'll be okay. Where are the kids?"

"When they took Tony to surgery, I made them go get something to eat, then go home and take care of the house and pack bags for me and Tony." Her arm bumped the lump in his jacket pocket. "What's that?"

In the high emotion of the moment, Lance almost laughed. He pulled out the baseball Keli had given him, which he'd stuck in his pocket at the last moment. "Part of my reeducation with Coach." He summarized Keli's lesson on balance.

Amanda turned the ball around in her hands, pausing

when she saw what he'd written about work. One eyebrow lifted, but she said nothing. Finally, she handed it back to him. "I'm sorry I took you away from that."

Lance stared at her. "Are you kidding?" He glanced at Tony. "This is more important than anything. Coach not only understands, he's praying for us." He pulled her to him, and she leaned heavily against him, closing her eyes with a long sigh.

"Coach not only understands, he's praying for us."

"I'm glad you came. Sometimes I wish I didn't need you so much."

Lance stilled, her words bothering him in a way he couldn't quite grasp. "Why?"

"Because you have so much on you with the company, especially since the buyout. I feel like we just add to that load."

Lance felt as if his heart had stopped. He gripped her, and Amanda's eyes opened in surprise.

"No," he said forcefully. "Don't say that. Don't even think it. The only reason I can deal with all that is because

I have you to come home to. You and the kids." He stroked her face. "I know it's been hard, and I've not been there. But that will be different. It's why I went to Coach, why you wanted me to go."

Slowly, she nodded. "We'll get through it."

They sat, silently holding each other, until two of the nurses came in and began to check Tony. One of them smiled gently at Amanda and Lance. "We'll be here a while if you want to take a break or get something to eat."

"I ate a while ago," Amanda said, nudging Lance toward the door. "You need to eat."

"I'm okay."

"Your stomach is growling. We've been here before. You know it'll be a while. Go eat."

The nurse nodded. "Seriously, this is going to take some time. Go. We'll find you if something changes."

Lance recognized the wisdom of it, even though he didn't want to leave, and he headed for the cafeteria. He felt numb, not hungry, but he knew all too well how exhausting hospital stays could be. He ate without tasting the food, his mind locked on his family.

How far off track have I gotten that she'd see herself and the kids as a burden? Do I really make them feel as if they're in my way?

Obviously yes.

Lance left the cafeteria as the numbness spread, and his feeling of isolation from his family, even from his coworkers, sank into his bones. He'd been so focused on making his company a success and proving to his new board that they'd been right to take a chance on him and his company, that he'd lost sight of anything else. Anything important.

Gail and I will be praying …

Coach was praying for them. So was Amanda. But he couldn't.

I have pushed God away too.

Back on the medical floor, Lance passed the family waiting room, paused, and went in. Empty at this late hour, the room's chill matched the chill he felt inside. A television flickered in a silent pantomime. On one corner table, a Gideon-placed Bible offered comfort to anxious families.

Lance sank into one of the chairs and picked up the Bible, rubbing one hand over the cover. His wife knew hers inside and out. His daughter and son listened to it regularly on their MP3 players.

But he didn't even know where to begin.

Grief washed over him, and Lance slid from the chair to his knees. Simple, plaintive words poured out of him.

"Lord, please help us. Heal Tony. Please don't take him from us. We need him. *I* need him. I need them. Help me to find my way home and back into their hearts. Guide me. Guide us." He took a ragged breath. "Heal us."

He could say nothing else. As eloquent as he could be in the boardroom, now … nothing. But Amanda always said God could hear your heart. He hoped that was true, now more than ever.

"Daddy?"

His head snapped up. Connie and Robert stood in the doorway, eyes filled with tears as they stared at their dad on his knees. Their faces were pinched with concern.

"Mama said you'd gone to eat …"

He struggled to stand. "I'm sorry," was all Lance could manage.

But it was enough. His children rushed to him, and he wrapped both of them in his arms, pulling them close.

"I'm sorry," he said again as he kissed the top of Connie's head and clutched Robert's shoulder. "I've been an idiot."

"Yes, you have," Connie whispered. Then she looked up at him and grinned. "We forgive you, Daddy, but don't do it again."

"I won't. Promise." He looked at Robert, abruptly realizing that his son was now at least an inch taller than he was. "You looked good out there at practice."

Robert's face flushed. "Thanks, Dad."

"Mr. Marshall?"

They all turned to the nurse standing in the doorway. "Is it Tony?"

She motioned for them to follow. "He's awake."

> "We forgive you, Daddy, but don't do it again."

The next two days were a blur. Tony, despite the doctor's worries, awoke with few complications. He remained woozy and a bit nauseous, but they knew that would fade soon. Amanda and Lance slept at the hospital, ever watchful, but forty-eight hours after his surgery, Tony woke them, begging for his soundboard … *and breakfast.*

The doctors wanted to keep Tony a couple more days. As Lance and Amanda shared lunch in the cafeteria, she told her husband that she wanted him to go back to Minnesota.

"I want you to finish what you started with Coach."

He started to protest, but she reached for his hand, squeezing it tightly. "Tony's going to be okay. We know that now. The rest of this stay will be routine. We've been through this before. Yes, I'd love to have you here, but I can't tell you how much the change I already see in you means to me. I love you, and I admit I can't wait to see where else this takes you … us."

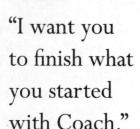

"I want you to finish what you started with Coach."

Lance agreed, and later that afternoon, he found himself back on a plane. Sitting next to the window, he turned the baseball over in his hands, looking at the phrase he'd written for work.

Now he understood exactly what a "win" would be for his family. He pulled out a pen and wrote: *family: that they know they are more important to me than anything. That we will be walking through life together, always.*

7

CLINT: SIMPLICITY

The Second Non-Negotiable

Despite his exhaustion from the hospital stay, Lance woke early the next morning, his mind churning with ideas for putting his daily "wins" into action.

He started by emailing each member of his leadership team, expressing how valuable they were to him as well as to the company. He spent extra time carefully crafting the email to Bryan. Lance had pushed Bryan hard both because of his value to the team and his potential.

Coach finally set his computer keyboard on top of the monitor and put the mug in its place. He nodded.

"The emails were a great start. Tell me more about your family."

Lance detailed the hospital visit, especially his promises to Amanda and his reconciliation with his children.

Coach grinned. "Connie sounds like she has you pegged."

"I think they both do. They're old enough to remember the old Dad, before I went off my rocker."

Coach chuckled. "Children are far more resilient than we realize sometimes. And smarter." He shifted in his chair and focused on Lance. "Ready for the next visit?"

Lance took a deep breath and held it a few seconds. "Yes."

Coach turned and braced a stack of papers with one hand, sliding one sheet out like a magician pulling a tablecloth from beneath a stack of dishes. He handed it to Lance, who stared at the stack of papers in astonishment.

"Remember Clint?"

Lance nodded, looking from the stack to the paper in his hand. "Absolutely. He was a year ahead of me, and the best receiver I ever had. Good baseball catcher, too. He went on to play pro ball in the minor leagues."

"Stayed there. He's a manager now." Coach pointed at the paper. "Those are the directions to his park. He's expecting you."

"So am I the only player who hasn't stayed in touch?"

Coach simply motioned to the paper. "Go. And in the morning, let's meet at Dottie's for coffee instead of here. Be there at 5:30 a.m. Tomorrow's a longer drive for you, so you'll need to start early."

Lance left Coach's office, reading the driving directions as he walked. His destination wasn't far, and he pulled up to a park silent and cautiously winterized. Parts of the parking lot had been cordoned off for repaving, and the boarded-up concession stands reminded him of a house fortified for a storm. In the offices, however, activity buzzed efficiently, and an assistant showed Lance into Clint's office.

Clint stood and greeted Lance with the fierce hug of an old friend. At forty-six, Clint's buzz-cut hair showed only light touches of gray, and his wiry, muscled physique reminded Lance of the quick-moving receiver and catcher who'd helped the high school teams win several championships.

"You're still in good shape," Lance said as he sat in a comfortable chair in front of Clint's desk. "You look like you could still stretch a double into a triple."

Clint beamed. "As a matter of fact, I still do. Only now I do it when no one can see how slow I've gotten. One advantage of being a manager."

"Congrats on that, by the way. Not all of us managed to stay in sports."

"True. Although Coach's teaching remained seared into most of us."

Lance grimaced. "Except me."

Clint waved his hand dismissively. "Nonsense. It's there. You've just forgotten."

"Nonsense. It's there. You've just forgotten."

Glancing around the office, Lance noted how vastly different Clint's decor was from Keli's plush, luxurious office. This office spoke of a man focused on efficiency. The spare furnishings were practical and strong, as if they'd last a lifetime. Just as Keli's office showed signs of his personal life, the shelves behind Clint's office were lined with Little League trophies, finger paintings, and snapshots of his family. One larger portrait caught Lance's attention, and he pointed. "Is that your family?"

Clint reached behind him and grabbed the photo. He handed it to Lance.

"Sure is. Pride of my life."

Four children clustered around Clint and his wife, a simply dressed woman of gentle beauty. Lance squinted, noticing the almond-shaped eyes and round face of their younger daughter.

"Is she … ?" he began.

Clint nodded. "Down syndrome."

Lance resisted the urge to apologize. He knew how that response to Tony—"I'm sorry about your son"—irritated Amanda. She'd remain polite but explained that there was no need for regrets.

"How's her heart?"

Clint looked surprised for a second. "Good. She missed that complication."

Lance nodded and handed the picture back. "My son Tony arrived almost two months early." He summarized the medical issues they'd been through with Tony, including the shunt failure.

Clint replaced the photo on the shelf. "Coach mentioned a health issue, but not the details. No regrets?"

"None. Except for all the times I hear about a father of a special-needs child who's left his marriage and family."

Clint let out a long breath. "Tell me about it. They don't understand how much you can learn about yourself and about being a man from these kids. I have learned so much from Maddie. She's even helped me be a better coach."

Curiosity made Lance sit a little straighter. "How so?"

"She's a walking, talking example of Coach's non-negotiable of simplicity."

"Tell me more."

"That's what we're here to talk about. Simplicity. Trying to remain a simple man in a complex world. Not easy. But by focusing on the basics, sticking to them, you can achieve clarity in your vision and your process."

Clint continued. "When I watch Maddie, I see a child who has few distractions in her world. She sets her mind on one thing, and little else interferes until she's done. Same way with coaching."

He stood up and walked to a window overlooking the ball field, motioning for Lance to follow. They watched as players and coaches wandered out onto the deck, many of them still stretching and warming up muscles.

"I require players and coaches to be FAT."

"Wrong time of year for spring training, isn't it?"

Clint laughed. "True. Many of these guys only stay indoors this time of year. But we have a long season, and not all the games are played in summer weather. So any time the temps rise high enough, we head outdoors. That's just one way I require players and coaches to be FAT."

"Say what? FAT?"

Clint nodded in amusement. "Sorry. We're used to the term around here. It's an acronym. Stands for *Faithful, Available,* and *Teachable.* Before we sign any player to a contract or hire a coach, he must have those characteristics." He turned. "Let's go down to the field."

Clint led Lance through the building, into the locker room, and out onto the field, explaining as they walked.

"For a player—or coach—to be Faithful, they must fully trust the organization, understanding that we have their best interests at heart, not only as players, but as people. And they need to give as well as receive. They will need to be Available, to be willing to make time to be the best they can for the team as well as for their families and communities.

"Stands for *Faithful*, *Available*, and *Teachable*."

"To achieve these two, they'll need to have a Teachable spirit, or they have no shot. They can't come in thinking they know everything there is to know about baseball. Too many players show up on our doorstep thinking they learned all they need to know in high school or college. Too many coaches and players think that whatever they learned earlier in their careers is sufficient. John Wooden, the legendary UCLA basketball coach, once said that what separates the great coaches from the average ones are the coaches who don't think they know it all.

"A coach's job is to help an individual or a team get to a level that they cannot achieve by themselves."

"You see, Lance, coaches make that mistake; after they win a couple of titles or have some success, they think they have it all figured out. This isn't just about results or winning; it's about life. It's about getting back to the basics, simple principles that most of us forget over time. Mature coaches aren't distracted by the tyranny of the urgent. They understand what they can control and what they can't. We call that 'controlling the controllables.' Great coaches and athletes understand what they can control and what they can't, and they simply let go of the things they can't.

They stay focused on the simplicity of who they are and the fact that they're there to help people get to the next level."

Clint paused for a second and went on. "I can't say that enough. *A coach's job is to help an individual or a team get to a level that they cannot achieve by themselves.* When that job is done properly, the wins come as a result."

Clint and Lance wandered up into the bleachers and sat, watching as the drills became more intense. Clint gestured at the first-base coach. "That is a remarkable man. After his playing career ended, he began coaching. He had many opportunities to coach with other major league clubs, but he was looking for something special. He wanted to be a part of an organization that was about more than winning. When he heard about our philosophy of coaching and development, he called me. Took a huge pay cut to come here and let go of all the unhealthy things the culture of pro baseball was selling in regard to winning."

"Letting go is not my specialty," Lance said.

Clint chuckled. "Yeah, I remember when you tried to tell Coach what plays to run."

Lance replied, "Coach had a few things to say about that."

"We were all surprised he let you play that week!" Clint paused, his voice softening. "Coach said you had some issues at work."

"Yeah, you could say that."

"My guess is that your team sees you as their control-freak boss. They're scared of you and for their jobs. No one maximizes their potential or performance in a state of fear, and you can't *force* anyone to do something they don't want to. Not your employees, not your new owners.

"You need to let go of the nonessentials and focus on the controlling variables. Focus on the only two things you really can control: your Attitude and your Effort."

"You make it sound so simple."

"Focus on the only two things you really can control: your Attitude and your Effort."

Clint stood and slapped Lance on the shoulder. "It is, my friend. You're the one making it complicated. Just remember. Attitude and Effort. Over the years, we've found that 90 to 99 percent of the problems we had with employees in the organization, including the players, boiled down to those two things. Lance, I have always told my assistant coaches that I will never come in and take over their position and start coaching their people. That is their job. But if I ever see a bad attitude or a poor effort, I will coach that immediately. Those two things are a non-negotiable in regard to the simplicity of our ball club, and that simplicity is what our success hinges upon."

An assistant beckoned Clint to the pressroom. He turned back to Lance. "I'm sorry, it looks as though the media is calling. Feel free to hang around as long as you like. Remember, Lance, you can't give away what you don't possess yourself. Strive to be a simple man in a complex world. Attitude and Effort."

On the drive back, Lance kept repeating those two words over and over, applying them in his mind to the events of the last month. Right after the buyout, everyone had worked hard, but lately getting his people to go above and beyond had become a trial. Understanding finally, Lance pulled over to the side of the road, took out his pen, and wrote *Attitude* and *Effort* on the baseball.

Then Lance picked up the phone and called Terri. He told his incredulous assistant to shut down the office on Friday and send everyone home and set up a company-wide meeting for Monday morning.

He pulled back onto the highway, energized and brainstorming even more about how he could emphasize Attitude and Effort in every facet of his life. He knew his world was about to change significantly.

DR. KESS: THE THREE-DIMENSIONAL LEADER

The Third Non-Negotiable

The workday started early, as it does in most small towns. Dottie's opened at five, and the smell of hot biscuits and bacon filled the air. A table reserved for local farmers buzzed with early-morning gossip, the talk ranging from crop futures and weather conditions to the latest episode of *American Idol.* A coffee station just inside the door invited customers to grab a cup and take a seat.

Lance snagged a booth early, downing his first cup and a hot biscuit before the sun rose. As Coach entered and settled into the seat across from him, Lance got up to pour his mentor a cup and refill his own. As he set the pot down, his phone buzzed three times in quick succession, signaling the arrival of three new emails. Lance stopped, setting the cups on the stand. He clicked through the emails, his chest tightening at the news they brought.

Three of his managers were all struggling with the same client, the same problem. One of the emails contained the entire exchange with the client, and Lance could read the anger between the lines of each message. The client wanted to end the negotiations; his managers wanted to let him walk.

A surge of anger shot through Lance, as if nothing in the last few days had changed. How dare they tear down the rapport he'd built! Did they not realize how important this was, how desperately they needed to grow in that territory? This should have been a coup, not a disaster!

Without looking up from the phone, Lance swung back toward the coffee stand. He stopped abruptly, thudding into someone. Hot coffee showered over Lance's left arm and hand, soaking his sleeve and cell phone.

He jumped back with an enraged growl, shaking his arm and staring down at the phone. "Why don't you watch where you're going, you stupid—"

He stopped, looking up into the eyes of a woman who could have been his grandmother. White curls looped around the frames of her glasses, and her cheeks flushed with embarrassment as she looked from him to her spilled coffee on the floor.

"I'm sorry," she muttered.

Every ounce of rage drained from Lance. *What have I done?*

"No, ma'am. You've done nothing. I'm sorry. I wasn't looking up." He bent and scooped her cup up, tossing it into the trash. "Let me get you another cup."

"No," she mumbled, her expression still a bit stunned. "I don't think I could drink it now."

"Let me help you …" Lance said.

Her eyes finally focused on him. "I'm old, young man. Not helpless. And you need to learn some respect."

"Yes, ma'am." He watched her leave, then looked over at Coach, who'd observed the incident with a wry grin.

"One step forward and two steps back, Lance?"

Now Lance's cheeks heated with embarrassment. "Seems like it."

Coach sipped his coffee. "Right. So did you throw a touchdown the first time you threw a pass?"

Lance leaned back. "Of course not."

"Then give yourself a break. Changing direction in your life is not like driving a car or sailing a boat. You can't just move the gibe from one side to the other and stay the course. You're going to slip. You're going to fail. The objective is to get back up and continue the process. How did it go with Clint?"

Lance paused as the waitress appeared and they ordered breakfast. Then Lance summarized his meeting with Clint and his plans for implementing new strategies at work that would focus more on attitude and effort. He pointed at

"You're going to slip. You're going to fail. The objective is to get back up and continue the process."

his phone, sharing the messages. "I realized after I tried to run over that lady that I need to change so that I can respond to situations like that properly, without thinking about it."

"And your managers?"

"Same thing. I ran into her because I was so angry at them. Without realizing it, I lashed out. Unfortunately, she was in the way."

Coach nodded. "Like your family is in the way."

Lance stared, astonished.

Coach sipped his coffee. "Well, that's a better reaction than I think I would have gotten a few days ago. Surprise is better than rage."

"You think my family is in my way?"

"Not me. Them."

"Remember there are only three things you can do when you make a mistake: Admit It, Fix It, and Don't Repeat It."

Lance took a deep breath, Amanda's words echoing in his head: *I feel like we just add to that load.*

"I'm working on that."

"Just don't stop, and remember there are only three things you can do when you make a mistake: Admit It, Fix It, and Don't Repeat It."

Lance grinned. "I won't. And I'm going to email my managers after breakfast, talk to them about Attitude and Effort, and encourage them to focus on the solution, not the screaming match."

"What would you have done before this trip?"

"Stepped in. Taken over. Fixed everything."

"To what effect?"

Lance sniffed, not wanting to say it. "It would have demoralized them and made the client disrespect them."

"You're not their father, Lance. You're their leader. Their coach. If you want them to trust you and be loyal to you, you have to capture their hearts and earn their trust. Lance, consistency in your behavior will breed trust, and trust will breed loyalty. This, as well as focusing on process, is key."

They paused as the waitress brought food and more coffee. As she left, Coach bowed his head in silent grace over his meal. Lance sat still, watching, once again struck by Coach's quiet, steady faith.

"Speaking of being a heart capturer," Coach announced even before he looked up, "today I'm sending you to see a really good friend of mine. Dr. Kess has been coaching coaches for more than twenty years. He's a professor at the university, and you're going to attend one of his classes this morning. A master's-level course on reaching the twenty-first-century athlete." He reached for his coffee cup. "Trust me, it's not the same game it used to be."

Lance returned to his room to change clothes and freshen up before he headed out. He also made a few notes about his client, then called Terri. She linked Lance and his three managers in a conference call, and Lance spoke calmly about the account and the client, encouraging them to brainstorm solutions, leaving the blame in the closet. "I hired you because you're capable of dealing with situations like this. Show me what you can do."

The call made him run late, but he felt an unexpected sense of pleasure and pride at the eager brainstorming they'd shared, and he'd hung up feeling they would rectify the problem.

An hour later, Lance drove onto the university campus and found the building and room number Coach had given him. Class had been in session for more than ten minutes when he peered through the door, but Dr. Kess motioned for him to come inside. Lance felt awkward as he found a seat, and he noticed some of the students shifting uncomfortably as well.

Dr. Kess appeared thin, but his clear voice was firm, and his energetic actions made him seem to bounce about in front of the room. *Wiry*, Lance thought, *not frail.*

"Ladies and gentlemen, this is Lance Marshall. He's auditing our class today. He is not an official of the university and therefore has no effect on your grades or my pay. So no need to be nervous at his presence."

Most of the students grinned or snickered, and the tension in the room eased. A couple of them even gave him reassuring glances of welcome. Coach had told Lance the class was a master's level, but he still found it startling to see how many of the students were older, some in their forties and fifties.

"Today's athlete is quite different from the way we were as children. Even children raised in the turbulent seventies and eighties still offered up trust to coaches and teachers simply because of the positions they held. They extended loyalty to coach and team without question. But with the advent of the Internet and more betrayals by authority figures than we can count, our students have been raised in a jaded world. The time of blind obedience has passed. They don't trust without reason, and while motivation by fear will work, it'll only last for short periods of time. This is because

"Remember, when I refer to mental toughness, I am referring to a person's ability to be comfortable with being uncomfortable."

the twenty-first-century athlete is not as mentally tough as we might hope. Remember, when I refer to mental toughness, I am referring to a person's ability to be comfortable with being uncomfortable. For a variety of reasons we will discuss another day, they have been conditioned to respond to difficult situations in two ways: with a flight response or by blaming someone else. In other words, the twenty-first-century athlete has been conditioned to change lanes when things get tough rather than stay the course and work through it. Lastly, we all need to feel safe, secure, and significant every day, or we will begin to lose hope and our motivational levels will decrease. People today don't care what you know until they know how much you care about them."

Dr. Kess pointed to an image of a pyramid divided into three sections that was projected on the front wall of the classroom. A similar pyramid sat on his desk, not much bigger than a paperweight.

"Today's coaches must be three-dimensional. You must go beyond being able to teach the fundamentals of the game. Today you must reach them body, mind, and spirit. Let's look at this closer."

He reached for the pyramid on his desk and separated the three pieces. "This bottom piece here, this is the largest section. This represents the fundamentals of the game. You must be intimately familiar with the basic principles and forms of your sport and possess up-to-date knowledge of truths and facts about it. You'll need to have a technical competency yourself and be able to cast a vision for your team, develop that vision, and take it through to implementation. And, truthfully, with the vast amount of knowledge available to us today, there's no excuse for incompetence in the fundamentals. But all this is just the foundation."

He set that piece on the desk and picked up the next one.

"Here … this is the second dimension of being a three-dimensional coach: the athlete's mind. You will need to understand the psychology of this young person and how he or she relates to the rest of the world. More than ever before, motivating a young athlete requires developing an understanding of the person inside the uniform. Current research shows that more than 90 percent of motivation today depends on the relationship between coach and player."

Dr. Kess picked up a remote control and clicked it. A page from Facebook reflected from the back wall.

"One of my students told me he has seven hundred and fifty-nine 'friends' on Facebook but only five real relationships. He goes home to his parents almost every weekend because he shares little with the people in his dorm and on his team. As always, people crave connection, real relationships with others. They know how powerful relationships can be and how shallow their world can be."

> "They want you to be someone they can trust and believe in who will challenge them to new levels."

Dr. Kess continued. "Don't get me wrong; they won't be looking to you to be their 'buddy.' You're their coach. They want you to be someone they can trust and believe in who will challenge them to new levels. They will expect you to lead them and know how to provide feedback and discipline when they screw up. So if you want to motivate your team members, you need to develop a relationship with them. Only then can you inspire them to persist and pursue when they want to quit. Only then can you help them achieve what they don't think possible."

Setting the second section aside, Dr. Kess picked up the smaller top section. "This, my friends, is the smallest but most important dimension. This is the heart of the athlete."

He turned it around in his hands. "Fragile yet infinitely strong. Easy to break, but if captured in the right way, through a process built on trust and daily care, the heart bond between a coach and his or her athletes can inspire both to greater heights than either imagined.

> "Great coaches are easy to please and hard to satisfy."

"Great coaches are easy to please and hard to satisfy. If you've earned the right to speak into your players' lives, then they will absorb everything you can offer, and they will not resent you when you give them feedback on their progress. They will embrace the core principles you teach them so intensely that these principles will become second nature. If you can capture their hearts, you will have no trouble with motivation or performance execution. Not to mention, team chemistry will go through the roof! They'll have fun and they'll win, and they won't even realize that you've led them to skills that will serve them the rest of their lives."

Dr. Kess set the pyramid top down.

"Take out a piece of paper, please," he said.

The students rustled through notebooks to pull out paper, and a young man next to Lance handed him a fresh sheet. Lance pulled a pen from his pocket and waited.

Dr. Kess switched back to the slide of the pyramid. "Draw this on your paper. Then I want you to put an X on the pyramid, representing where you think you are as a coach." He waited as they drew, then continued. "Now place a check mark where you think your athletes would put you."

A few groans echoed around the room. Lance stared at his pyramid, well aware of where his employees, his "team," would probably place him. He knew most of his employees respected his skills and his goals. But as a motivator, a coach … a heart capturer?

Not so much.

Dr. Kess cleared his throat. "This next part may be hard on some of you. Where would your spouse or significant other say you stood on the pyramid? Draw a circle where you think he or she would put you."

Lance desperately wanted to put the circle representing his wife in the top portion of the pyramid. She loved him, of course, but was he capturing her heart?

I wish I didn't need you so much. And Amanda's response to Connie's accusation: *he knows what he missed.*

Lance looked up at Dr. Kess's pyramid. *They want you to be someone they can trust and believe in.*

Motionless, Lance realized that Amanda didn't believe she could rely on him. He'd lost her trust in his being there when she needed him.

Dr. Kess continued, "Now if you have children at home, put a plus sign where they would say you are on the pyramid."

All of a sudden, Dr. Kess's class couldn't end soon enough.

9

COACH O QUARTERBACK SCHOOL: THE POWER OF SPEAKING GREATNESS

The Fourth Non-Negotiable

The next morning, Lance arrived at Coach Moore's office before anyone else did, pacing impatiently on the sidewalk in front of the school. Coach got out of his ancient pickup with a tall cup of coffee in one hand, and his eyebrows arched when he saw Lance. Then he merely grinned and motioned Lance inside.

"How did it go with Amanda?"

"Sometimes I wonder if I knew back when I was

sixteen years old how amazing she really is," Lance replied.

Coach moved a stack of papers and set the cup down on his desk. "No. You were sixteen. You had no idea how astonishing and strong a grown woman could be. Of course, she wasn't exactly all that mature yet either."

"I told her about the pyramid and Dr. Kess's ideas. The self-test. And I apologized for taking her and the kids for granted, especially her work with Tony. She's so strong and efficient with him, completely accepting that he'll never leave home and mature the way Connie and Robert will."

"He'll be eighteen soon and out of the special-needs education system. Have you talked about transition services for him?"

Lance closed his eyes a moment. "I haven't. Amanda has. She keeps trying to talk to me, but I can't deal with it."

Coach looked at him silently.

Lance sighed. "I know. I can't let her do this alone."

"I don't remember you having a hard time talking to people. Even when you said some pretty strong things, you said them without a lot of hesitation."

"Yeah, well, this time I'm trying to say the *right* things. Maybe that's why I'm wandering off into left field."

Coach grinned. "I think today's visit will help you with that. Do you know where Coyote Ridge Park is? It was built some time after you left."

Lance nodded. "I've passed it a few times since I got back."

"Go in the front entrance and circle around to the back. You'll see an open field at the back where a guy will be working with a young boy, tossing a football back and forth."

"Okay."

"That's Coach O. Jed Olson. One of the best collegiate coaches I've ever met. He does something else for a living these days, but he still gives private quarterback lessons to a few kids throughout the year. He can take a good player and turn him into a great one. Even NFL coaches and players have hired him."

"What's his secret?"

"That's what you're about to find out. Don't interrupt if he's in the middle of a lesson. He knows you're coming, and he'll get to you as soon as he can."

"This will help me with Amanda?"

"And Robert and Connie, and every employee you've ever hired. And come back here when you're finished. Gail wants to see you tonight. I'll take you over to the house."

Lance headed out, pulling into the park about fifteen minutes later. He followed the drive past a picnic shelter and an expansive playground. A lake sparkled in the sun, and a family with four children fed eager, noisy ducks and geese. Tennis courts gave way to a broad field bordered by giant oaks. Two cars sat in the narrow lot, and behind them two men casually tossed a football back and forth as a young boy listened closely to one of them.

Lance parked and got out, and the man next to the boy nodded at him.

"Be with you in a bit," he called out.

Lance waved back an agreement and leaned against the hood of his car. Even at this distance, Lance could see that the kid paid seriously close attention to Coach O's words, nodding occasionally. Coach O would show him something, explain it, model it, and then he would have the young boy throw the ball back to his dad.

Finally, Coach O called to his pupil's father, "Take a break, John. Josh is going to show me what he can do."

John nodded, then walked over to Lance as the boy ran out a distance, the ball tucked in at his side. John stuck out his hand. "I'm John. You must be Lance."

A little surprised, Lance nodded.

"Jed told me you were coming. He talked to Coach Moore this morning. He's the one who convinced Jed to work with Josh."

"Why didn't he want to work with your son?"

John crossed his arms and focused on his son. "Josh is good, but I know he can be better. But at ten, he's younger than most of the athletes Jed works with."

"Ten is pretty young. My son plays quarterback, but at ten it was still all about going to Dairy Queen after games."

John paused. "Let me back up a bit. A few years ago, a Fortune 500 company I'd helped start was poised to turn global. A shake-up at the executive level left me less than thrilled, so I knew I needed to move on, take some time, and figure out what came next. In the meantime, I began coaching my son's football team and became fascinated by what these kids could accomplish. We had a group of

THE LEGACY BUILDER

solid, enthusiastic youngsters, even though only one had exceptional athletic ability. Nonetheless, we were able to compile a 12–1 record, including preseason and postseason. We went on to win our version of the 'Super Bowl,' not because I'm that great a coach, but because these young players have an astonishing will to work hard and have fun while executing well. I mean, we only lost one fumble the entire season."

"Impressive," Lance said.

"The success of this team started me wondering what a kid could accomplish if he had coaches who understood the intricacies of a particular position, like Jed does with quarterbacks. Joshua was one of the quarterbacks on our team. I wanted to see how he would develop under the tutelage of a true quarterback coach. I began to ask around in coaching circles, and multiple recommendations led me to Jed. In fact, they told me, 'You probably can't get this guy, but if you can, he is the best around at developing kids.'"

"He does this for a living?"

John shook his head. "Not at all, although he could if he wanted to. He only works with a few quarterbacks a year—says it fills the football void in his life. Jed has held multiple positions as quarterback coach, offensive coordinator, and head coach at the collegiate level. I had to make a lot of calls to convince him to work with Josh, because he usually works with young men at the high school or college level. In fact, the youngest he had worked with previously was thirteen. I finally convinced him to meet with Josh under the agreement that we would meet just once and see how things went.

"I went to our first meeting expecting Jed to work with Josh on three-step drops and correct his throwing mechanics. Instead, we spent the first thirty minutes on the proper stance under center and the last fifteen minutes talking about leadership and the type of leader Josh should aspire to be."

Lance stared at John. "The kind of leader he wanted to be? He's ten."

John ran one hand through his hair. "I think part of Jed's success is that he teaches to their level but isn't afraid to challenge them. In retrospect, I think he was testing Josh, seeing if he had the maturity, patience, and aptitude to learn the details. And that's the way it went for a while.

In fact, we met half a dozen times before Josh was allowed to throw the ball more than ten yards. I expected Josh to get bored, but he continues to be excited about these lessons. He *always* leaves energized."

"So how does he look as a player? Has he improved since you started these?"

"Honestly, I didn't think it would happen this quickly, but yes. Josh's progress has been significant. Not only does the ball look as if it jumps off Josh's hand without effort, but his manner changed significantly. He's matured and now possesses a quiet confidence and calm that was never there before."

John shifted, pulled a pair of sunglasses out of his pocket, and slid them on. "I couldn't quite put my finger on it at first, but there's something significantly different about the way Jed coaches. After about a dozen sessions the difference became apparent ... it's the way he *speaks* to Josh. Not just what he says, but the tone he uses. Also, Jed's sequence of instructions, criticisms, and encouragement is intentional and just as important. This technique transformed my son. I had to learn more about it. When I discussed what I'd noticed with Jed over a cup of coffee, he told me he was using an approach he called 'Speaking Greatness,' and that through this process you could capture the heart of the athlete."

John gave a slight shrug. "I didn't know what he meant. He explained that once you captured the heart, the desired performance would follow. As we continued our discussion, I was overcome with the mixed emotions of regret and excitement. Regret that I had not been exposed to this approach or used it more broadly in my entire life with my business career, my children, or my wife. But I was also excited that I, hopefully, have another forty-plus years to 'Speak Greatness' into those I encounter."

John waved at Josh, who returned the gesture. "You know what's even better?"

"'Speaking Greatness,' and that through this process you could capture the heart of the athlete."

"Tell me," Lance replied.

"I've discovered that while 'Speaking Greatness' is great for the recipient, the true benefit comes in how God works in the heart of the person who is doing the speaking. When you speak greatness to others, you benefit as well, and in ways you can't imagine. My wife says that once you start speaking greatness at home, you will never stop. You will never go back to how you used to speak to people. It's amazing."

"A reflective effect."

John grinned as he pushed away from the car. "More than you can dream."

He stepped forward to greet his son, who glowed from the morning's effort.

"Did you see, Dad?"

"Every second." John put his arm around Josh's shoulder. "You ready to show your mom?"

"My wife says that once you start speaking greatness at home, you will never stop."

"You bet!" He scrambled for the car, as much a ten-year-old boy as a quarterback.

John shook Jed's hand. "Thanks again. Next week?"

"Absolutely."

Jed stood next to Lance, the football tucked under one arm, as they watched father and son drive away. Jed pulled a towel out of his car and draped it around his neck. "Let's stand in the shade."

They left the parking lot and headed for the ring of trees at the field's edge.

"John been talking your ear off?" Jed asked.

Lance chuckled. "He's definitely impressed with the work you've done with Josh."

"Josh is a good kid. He's got a deep, natural talent, but mostly he needed encouragement. A reminder—lots of reminders—that he has greatness inside him. And it is my job to help him discover it."

"He *is* only ten."

"Oh, yeah. But I think John has learned almost as much about being a coach and leader as Josh has about being a quarterback."

Lance turned to face Coach O, who was at least two inches taller. "I suspect he'd agree with you on that."

"He just needed to learn to do less pushing and do more leading, more encouraging."

"How so?"

Coach O paused, peering at Lance intently. "Coach Moore said you'd already visited Dr. Kess."

"Yes."

"So you understand the three-dimensional pyramid. Fundamentals, understanding the psychology of motivation, and capturing the heart?"

"Intellectually, yes. In practice, I haven't exactly hit the end zone."

Coach O snorted a laugh. "Coach Moore also said you could laugh at yourself."

"More in the last few days than the last few months. My sense of humor took a hit like everything else good in my life. I've not been a great guy to hang out with lately."

"Said some harsh things to important folks?"

"Just about everyone."

Coach O nodded. "People forget that there's life and death in the power of the tongue. It's absolutely *not* true that words don't hurt. They *can* hurt, and they can change a life. You know that the basic definition of a coach is 'someone who helps an individual or a team get to a level they couldn't get to by themselves.'"

"I've heard that a couple of times this week."

"And it's true, but it goes even a step further—that's not only a coach's job; it's a leader's job and a parent's job to discover the gifts of their athletes, employees, and children and help them to flourish. Fan the flames."

"How?" Lance asked.

"For one thing, don't focus on what they can't do; focus on what they can do."

"People forget that there's life and death in the power of the tongue."

"People do make mistakes."

"Sure they do. We all do. The kids I coach do, and when they make them, I critique them and teach them how to correct them. I tell them, okay, you made a mistake—good, mistakes are how we learn. Then I tell them there are only three things they can do when they make a mistake: Admit It, Fix It, and Learn from It. When they hear that, all of a sudden they're more motivated because they don't worry about failing. They know it's part of the learning process. So we correct, but we focus on excellence and process. When we give feedback, we focus on the process, not results. Any idiot can state what the kid did wrong. We call this type of coach 'Coach Obvious.' That kind of coach simply restates what the kid did. For example, a kid misses a tackle, and the coach runs over and screams, 'Make the tackle' at the kid. Lance, today's athletes are smart, and they want their coach to help them fix the problem, not just restate results. When I give feedback to people, I practice a three-to-one ratio when critiquing performance. This means for every correction that you wish to make, you must tell them three specific things they're doing right first."

"That can't always be easy."

"No, it's not. Some kids need more work than others. But when you're correcting their mistakes *and* praising their successes, it has an amazing effect."

"Such as?"

"One, they know you are the real deal, that you're not just telling them what they want to hear. You have to remember, most of these kids have been getting trophies for just showing up. They yearn for authentic coaching and feedback. You fix as well as praise; you're not just telling them how good they are. They know it's not an empty compliment just to make them feel better. So they start to trust you."

Lance nodded, taking it in.

"Two, the more they trust you, the more they want to please you and not disappoint you. Remember, great coaches are easy to please and hard to satisfy."

Coach O moved the football from one hand to the other, absently twirling it.

"Lance, the ability to motivate someone to do something is about 90 percent trust. If you want me to do something, I need to be able to trust that you've got my back. You'll stand behind me when I do great, as well as when I fail. With your wife and your employees, if they've lost faith in your willingness to support them, then you've lost their trust. You can yell at them all day long, but that won't make them more inclined to work harder. Constant criticism and sarcasm tear down their spirit. It creates an environment of fear, and again, when people are in a state of fear, all they care about is survival, not performing at a high level."

Lance thought for a second about how criticism flowed so easily out of his mouth, both at work and at home.

"The ability to motivate someone to do something is about 90 percent trust."

"One of the things I learned working with these kids is that I need to have a transformational vocabulary. I need to use words that take them to another level. Here's an example. Say Josh is throwing out routes to receivers, and I say, 'Josh, that was a great pass, *but* …' What happens to everything I said before the word *but*?" Coach O asked.

"It's gone, forgotten, almost like you never said it."

"Correct. But what if I simply replace the word *but* with the word *now*? For example, 'Josh, that was a great pass; *now* I want you to try this!' You see, Lance, the word *now* is a transformational word. It inspires people to go to the next level in their performance. You still get the message across, you still critique and correct them, and you also challenge them to another level."

"It's all about the process."

"Exactly. And this works with everyone, not just athletes. I know this sounds radical because it's so far away from the way we've been taught to manage or to coach. But if you will 'Speak Greatness' at least five times a day— to your employees, your colleagues, your superiors—you'll see a difference immediately."

"John said it had a bit of a 'reflective' effect."

Coach O nodded. "Without a doubt. It's an intentional behavior that'll change you as much as the people to whom you're speaking."

"You make it sound really simple."

"Yep. Because the concept *is* simple. It's living it every day, stopping to think every time before you speak, that's harder. But it's definitely worth it."

Coach O pulled a marker from his pocket and wrote *THINK* across the side of the football. "Here. I want you to take this and put it in your office. You don't have to explain it if you don't want to. But you'll know that this isn't just the word *think*. The letters stand for 'True. Helpful. Inspiring. Necessary. Kind.' I challenge you to *think* before you speak." He handed Lance the football.

"Thanks. I just hope I can put all this into practice as well as you do."

Coach O slapped Lance on the shoulder. "I think you already have."

"I challenge you to *think* before you speak."

10

THE ASSISTANT COACH: VALUE PEOPLE OVER PRODUCTIVITY

The Fifth Non-Negotiable

The advice from Coach O's session swirled in Lance's mind as he headed back to the gym. He felt both overwhelmed and uplifted, and he couldn't quite believe that his time with Coach Moore had come to an end. Coach had been right—Lance had heard all this before, mostly when he'd been in high school. Everything felt familiar and right, like renewing an acquaintance with an old friend. Still, Lance was chagrined to realize that so little of it had "stuck."

He entered the school, his footsteps echoing off the walls as he turned down the hallway to the gym. Lance realized that his reluctance to leave ran deeper than mere nostalgia for his high school days, and he thought about Dr. Kess's words about safety and security. Here he felt both of those things. Here he felt cherished, and he knew he needed to rebuild those feelings for his own children.

Lance entered the coaches' anteroom and immediately saw that Coach Moore's office was dark and silent. He stopped, wondering if he'd misheard the time of their meeting.

"Lance?"

He turned, and Coach Doug Dawson waved from behind his desk, motioning for Lance to join him. Lance entered an office much neater than that of the head coach and sat down.

Coach Dawson opened a small refrigerator behind his desk and handed Lance a bottle of water, which he accepted gratefully. "Coach Moore got a call from the principal for some sort of conference. He'll be back in a bit. Have you learned a lot?"

Lance twisted off the lid. "More like relearned it. I can't believe how much I've forgotten."

Coach Dawson opened his own bottle. "Because you haven't been living it."

Lance looked closer at him. "How do you mean?"

"Do you value people over productivity?"

"I don't understand," Lance said, puzzled.

"Has Coach ever told you how we came to work together?"

Lance shook his head.

"Not surprised. That's like him. He respects everyone's privacy. Lets them tell their own stories."

"I thought he hired you here."

"Yes … and no." Coach Dawson shrugged one shoulder. "We've been at this school more than thirty-five years. Before that, Coach was briefly at a tiny school south of here, near the state line. He convinced them to hire me to coach and teach a couple of math courses. I was

"Do you value people over productivity?"

still a kid, barely out of school, and I thought I knew everything there was to know about winning."

Lance grinned. "Winning."

"Yeah, you hear it coming, don't you?"

"After these few days, yeah."

"Yep, I'd been on the job only a few months. One evening after practice, Coach pulled me aside and took out a pad and pencil. He said, 'All right, I want his name.' I stared at him. 'Whose name?' He licked the end of the pencil and prepared to write. 'The guy who told you that winning games is what this is all about. Whoever told you that winning, no matter the cost to your players and yourself, would make you a better coach. I want his name because I'm going to hunt that sucker down.'"

They both laughed before Coach Dawson continued. "That was the first time I'd ever heard anything about motivating kids through relationship by reaching their hearts and minds. I'd been taught that coaching was about technical skills and motivating players through fear." He paused. "That night he told me how much of his coaching philosophy wasn't new, just older principles he'd put back into place. He told me how he had hurt so many along the way, just for the sake of winning, and how he vowed he would never do that again. He got me on my feet not only as a coach, but also as a man."

"I can see why you'd be loyal."

Coach Dawson peered at Lance a moment. "Actually, I'm loyal more because he almost fired me the week of the state championship game."

Lance's eyes widened. "Say that again?"

Setting his water aside, Coach Dawson pulled his chair closer and braced his elbows on the desk.

"My father had been ill for six months. I'd made a dozen trips home to help my mom. It had been a rough season, but we'd made it to the championship game, in part because we never stopped encouraging our team on what they were doing right and fixing what they were doing wrong. Our team was loading the bus to the game when I got the call about my dad. They didn't think he'd last through the night.

"But I wasn't going to walk away from the team. I wasn't about to leave Coach. We'd worked so hard and deserved every reward. Finally, Coach said, 'Doug, there will be other championship games. I promise you that. But you will not have another father. This man taught you to throw a ball and be a man. He gave you a safe and secure place to grow up. He brought you into the world. You need to be there when he leaves it.'"

"You went?"

"No, not at first. I told Coach I could catch a red-eye flight after the game. He told me that if I didn't leave immediately, he would fire me and then hunt me down. So I left immediately. Incredibly, I made it home in time. I was there when my dad lost consciousness, and I was still there when he passed away. I wouldn't have been if I'd waited for that red-eye flight. And there *were* other championship games. Enough that folks now call Coach a legend. You see, Lance, we can talk coaching philosophies all day long, but Coach lived it out that night. He valued me and my family over the

"He brought you into the world. You need to be there when he leaves it."

program and a game. I am loyal to Coach because he lives these principles out every day. When Coach says, 'Value people over productivity,' he means it. To me, that's what makes Coach a legend. Not the winning. If you put what you have learned into action every day, you'll see exactly what I mean."

Lance started to respond, but Coach Dawson's gaze shifted up and behind him, and Lance knew Coach Moore had returned. He stood and turned.

"Hiding out?"

"Hardly," Coach Dawson said. "I was just picking his brain a bit about coaching philosophies and what he's learned this week. Thought I might have missed something."

Coach Moore nodded at his assistant as if sharing a private joke, then motioned for Lance to follow him. "Come on, champ. My wife has already let me know that she's tired of holding up dinner because of us. Lock up, would you, Doug?"

"I'll take care of it."

Lance and Coach Moore headed for the parking lot. "Why don't you follow me in your car? Gail's dinner always makes me so sleepy, I don't want to leave the house after we eat."

"No problem."

"Don't get lost."

"Never again."

Coach grinned at him as he opened the door on his old pickup and got in, slamming it behind him.

As he followed Coach toward his home, Lance couldn't get Doug Dawson's story out of his head, nor the obvious connection to his own life. Pulling out his cell phone, he dialed Terri's personal number.

When she answered, he said simply, "Tell me what's going on with Bryan. The whole story."

11

ENDGAME: BECOMING A LEGACY BUILDER

Coach Moore and his wife, Gail, lived in the same renovated farmhouse they'd purchased thirty-five years before. The broad backyard had been a practice field for thousands of young players over the years, and Gail still loved to entertain on the deck behind the house. The men could smell the food when they got out of the car, and Coach had just started explaining Gail's new recipe for grilled vegetables when Amanda rounded the corner of the house.

Lance stopped, eyes wide and disbelieving, as she trotted toward him. "Surprise!" she whispered as she pulled him into a hug. Lance returned the hug, holding her as if she might float away when he let go.

"Wow!" she said when he finally released her. "I need to send you out of town more often."

"Never," he said, his voice teasing. "You're never getting rid of me, never ever again."

She laughed, slipping her arm around him as they walked to the back of the house. "Gail called me, invited me up. She said you'd changed a lot over the last few days. According to Coach."

"I think I have. I know I have a lot to work on. Everyday stuff."

Coach, who had walked on ahead of them, now offered up cups of hot chocolate as Gail began forking steaks from the large brick grill, plopping them onto a large platter. "I wasn't about to wait for you boys to do the grilling tonight. I'm starved!"

"Let me get that." Lance grabbed the hefty platter and carried it to the picnic table, setting it near a large Dutch oven brimming full of grilled vegetables. The heat from the open fire of the grill wafted over them, pushing away the chill of the autumn night as they settled down on the wooden benches.

"Lance, would you say grace?" Coach asked.

Lance stared at him a moment. He'd not said grace in a long time. In fact, the only prayers he'd muttered recently had been ones of desperation at the hospital. He glanced at Amanda, who nodded her encouragement.

Gail's soft voice made it unanimous. "Just speak from your heart, dear."

They bowed their heads, and Lance cleared his throat. "Lord, thank You for this food and for the people You put in our lives. May we never take them for granted. Amen."

> "Lord, thank You for ... the people You put in our lives."

"Amen," Coach said. "That didn't sound like you'd wandered *that* far from Him."

"I guess not."

Gail passed him a bowl of salad. "What did you learn from your session with Coach O?"

Lance glanced from her to Coach Moore. "Tag teaming me?" he teased.

"Tandem teaching," his mentor responded with a smile. "We do make a good team."

"So do you and Amanda," Gail said.

"I agree." Lance brushed his wife's arm. "And I know I'd rather not ever repeat the past year."

"Amen!" Amanda agreed.

Lance filled them in on the high points from the day's session, ending with the somber news he'd gotten from Terri. "Bryan's always been my best man. But he's really failed a lot lately. Terri told me his wife has multiple sclerosis."

"Oh, no," Amanda whispered.

"Obviously, things are tough emotionally and financially. She's receiving treatments, but she has a lot of bad days. She had to quit her job, and there are times she can't even take care of their kids."

"They have three little ones," Amanda said to Gail and Coach.

"I have to find a way to help. I told Terri to find a nanny service that can fill in when they need it. We'll pick up the tab. And we'll set up Bryan so he can work from home as a satellite employee when he needs to. I hope that'll ease some of their stress."

Coach exchanged a knowing look with Gail. "So you think you can follow the path of a three-dimensional leader?"

Lance nodded. "I do. It's a challenge, but I know I can turn things around."

"Just keep that pyramid in front of you."

"I definitely have that in mind."

"That's a start, but I meant that in a more concrete way."

"How so?"

"Test yourself, just like you did in Dr. Kess's class. Draw the pyramid on a piece of paper and put your X on there, then the circle for Amanda and the plus sign for the kids, then a check for your employees. I encourage my coaches as well as my players to do that on a regular basis. Once a week even. Or a month. It's a simple thing that can keep you on track and help you apply Coach O's advice of 'Speaking Greatness' into people in every direction. Even if you do nothing else, those will keep you focused on the process and on your own attitude and effort."

"I could ask you about them," Amanda offered.

Gail shook her head. "No. Don't push him to do it. Has to be from his heart." She glanced lovingly at her husband. "Besides, you'll know when he's not doing it, just like you did this time." She turned back to Lance. "Do you have a pen on you?"

Lance nodded and pulled one from his shirt pocket. Gail handed him one of the paper napkins.

"I want you to write the name of someone who's made a major impact on your life—in a positive way."

Lance scribbled the name.

"Now, tell me one or two things this person did so consistently that it captured your heart and made this person an important part of your life."

Lance hesitated, then took a deep breath. "He was so calm and even-keeled. His teaching never varied. He challenged me and cared about me as a person, not just as a player."

Gail nodded. "Then you need to realize that you are that person's legacy. His lessons will live on in you, and

"It's now time for you to decide what your legacy will be and how you'll pass it on."

then they'll be passed from this generation to the next. It's now time for you to decide what your legacy will be and how you'll pass it on."

Lance looked down at the napkin, silently reading the name of the man across the table from him.

Gail's soft voice continued. "You can write your legacy, dear, starting today. By taking all this in and changing the way you lead, the way you behave toward others, you can control what people will say about you ten minutes

"You can write your legacy, dear, starting today."

from now and a hundred years from now. I encourage you to start the process of building your legacy right now. And start with your beautiful wife and children at home."

Lance looked from Gail to Coach, who nodded his encouragement. Silent, Lance reached over and slipped his hand into Amanda's.

Two days later, Lance stood on the front porch of a modest ranch house, nervously shifting his weight from one foot to the other. He looked around, noticing that while the home could use some work, it was obviously well cared for and loved. He glanced down at his briefcase again, as if something about it might have changed in the last five seconds. Inside were the details on setting up a satellite office and the package from the nanny service. He prayed again that this would go well.

He rang the doorbell again. This time the door opened, and Bryan stared at his boss, a wary expression turning to fear in his eyes.

Lance cleared his throat. "Bryan, I'm here because I care about you, and our company would not be where it is today without your personal commitment to excellence, your loyalty, and your integrity. I have a plan to offer you, which I hope will be a win-win situation for all of us. We need to talk."

Bryan stared at him a moment, not quite believing him. Finally, he stepped back and invited Lance in.

Lance turned just before the door shut, looking at the baseball resting on the dash of his car. Since returning from his visit with Coach, he'd carried it everywhere. For now, it represented more than his need to specify the "win." It reminded him how much he'd changed. He would never speak—or lead—the same way again.

With a genuine sigh of relief, Lance shut the door to his past. Time to start a whole new way of life.

Time to start becoming a Legacy Builder.

THE 5
NON-NEGOTIABLES

1. Specify the Win
2. Simplicity in a Complex World
3. Be a 3-Dimensional Leader
4. The Power of Speaking Greatness^{SM}
5. Value People over Productivity

The 5 Non-Negotiables of the Legacy Builder

1. Specify the Win

- Maturity and balance go hand in hand.
- Specify daily what a "win" is for you at work and especially at home.
- Be process driven: things that are built to last are not built fast.
- You control the pace of leadership; don't let the pace control you.
- Focus on one thing at a time ... one day at a time.

2. Simplicity

- Are you a FAT leader?

  The criteria for an uncomplicated and qualified leader:

F—aithful: you fully trust the organization; you believe without seeing.

A—vailable: you make time to help yourself, others, and your community.

T—eachable: you possess a teachable and coachable spirit.

- "Control the Controllables"… Great coaches and leaders can discern what they can control and what they cannot.

- A coach or a leader's job is to take an individual or a team and get them to a level they cannot get to themselves.

- You can't give away what you do not possess yourself as a leader.

- Focus on Attitude and Effort daily; these two things control everything else.

3. Be a 3-Dimensional Leader

- The three dimensions of leadership

  Level 1—You are fundamentally sound, and you maintain high competency levels.

  Level 2—You know and practice the secrets

of motivating the twenty-first-century team member.

Level 3—You are a master relationship builder who is focused on capturing people's hearts while holding them accountable.

♦ Be mentally tough: the ability to be comfortable with being uncomfortable.

♦ Everyone needs to feel Safe, Secure, and Significant every day.

♦ Remember that 90 percent of motivation lies in relationship; people today want a leader who authentically cares about them both professionally and personally.

♦ Great leaders and coaches are easy to please and hard to satisfy.

♦ Earn the right to speak into your people by capturing their hearts.

4. The Power of Speaking Greatness^{SM}

♦ Realize that "life and death lie in the power of the tongue."

♦ Speaking Greatness^{SM} is a style of communication that allows a coach or a leader to motivate others by giving feedback in such a way that the individual listens to the instructions and/or criticisms and is not motivated by fear but by the desire to reach new levels and not disappoint the coach.

- Focus on the process or performance rather than just results.

- Practice a 3:1 ratio when giving feedback or critiquing your people.

- Utilize a transformational vocabulary and work on helping others discover what the "greatness" is that is inside of them—and fan that flame!

- There are only three things we all should do when we make a mistake:

  (1) Admit It

  (2) Fix It

  (3) Don't Repeat It; Learn from It

- **THINK** before you speak and ask these questions:

  T—rue: Is what I am about to say true? If not, do not speak.

  H—elpful: Is what I am about to say helpful, or will it escalate things?

I—nspiring: Is what I am about to say going to inspire them to the next level in their performance?

N—ecessary: Is what I am about to say truly necessary, or am I just wanting to hear myself talk?

K—ind: Is what I am about to say going to be received as a kind, professional comment? If not, bite your tongue and rephrase.

5. Value People over Productivity

- True Legacy Builders live out these principles daily.
- Emphasizing people always enhances performance.
- Don't buy the lie that winning or success will cure all your problems … Legacy Builders want to win, but that is secondary to winning in life.
- Keep your antennas up for opportunities to demonstrate to your family or team members that they are more valuable to you than what they can do for you.
- Remember that consistent behavior breeds trust, and trust breeds loyalty.

BUILDING YOUR
LEGACY NOW

I encourage you to do as Lance Marshall did and write down on the line below the name of someone who has had a positive, profound impact on your life. In fact, if it wasn't for this person, you might not be in the position in which you find yourself at this very moment.

The greatest leader I have ever personally known is:

_____

_____

The one thing that he or she consistently did to capture my heart was:

_____

_____

_____

Perhaps one day someone will read this book and write your name down as the leader who impacted him or her profoundly. However, the true measure of a Legacy Builder is what people learned from you and what they carry on from your life. What will people write and say that you did for them? I challenge you to start writing your legacy today by becoming a 3-Dimensional Leader who Speaks Greatness^{SM} into others!

ACKNOWLEDGMENTS

First, I wish to thank all the teachers and coaches I had over the years, teachers and coaches who are probably holding this book in disbelief. Please remember to keep teaching the bad kids too.

Truly many have contributed to the production of this book, and I have been humbled by the encouragement, support, and selfless help that so many have given to me. I would like to thank my parents, who long ago passed on, for the foundation of faith and values they instilled in me. Next, I wish to thank my wife, Marla, for bringing me back to those values and for her steadfast support of me as I dragged her all across this wonderful country. To my children, Colt, Connie, and Lance, for giving me the time to write and for putting up with a dad in process. I love you guys.

To those in my inner circle (who are many): I will not name names, as it would take too long, and I don't want to risk leaving someone out. I wish to thank you all for being Legacy Builders for me as we journey through life together. Iron does sharpen iron as one man sharpens another; this wouldn't have happened without you.

To my good friend Scotty Kessler, who showed me another way to lead and coach: thank you for taking the time to disciple me and for the freedom to share these principles with the world.

To Derek Fullmer, for giving me a model of what a true leader can be. Thank you for being a mentor who loves me, holds me accountable, and challenges me. What a blessing you are to me and my family.

To Ramona Richards, who made this story come alive: you are truly gifted. Thank you for putting up with an impatient ball coach.

To John Seiple, Doug Dawson, and Roy Dobie: thank you for your encouragement and help in allowing me to have the time to make this happen.

To Jerry Moore and all the coaches I have worked for

and with over the years: you are the inspiration for the characters in this book.

To all the players who have called me "Coach" over the years and have put into practice all the words in this book. For those I coached without these principles, I apologize and ask for your forgiveness, and for those who experienced these principles firsthand and had their lives transformed with me, thank you.

Finally, I wish to thank God for the principles and His Son who lived them out. The good in this book comes from Him, and whatever may be wrong with this book is on me … as it should be.

About the Author

ROD OLSON, or "Coach O," is the founder and CEO of the Coaches of Excellence Institute and the Coach O Consulting Group. Rod is a globally sought-after speaker, author, and advisor on twenty-first-century coaching, leadership, and parenting.

Following a twenty-year college coaching career, Rod has taught leadership at Quantico for the US DEA Leadership Academy, motivation at the USA Olympic Coaching Schools, and peak performance to the Pittsburgh Pirates major league baseball club. He has also mentored numerous CEOs of Fortune 500 companies, as well as many head coaches at all levels of sport.

Coach O lives with his wife and children near the beautiful Rocky Mountains in Denver, Colorado.

More information about Coach O can be found at www.RodOlson.org and www.coachesofexcellence.com.